PRAISE FOR 7

M000086646

The Ruby Rule is a timely and refreshing manual for day-to-day living that everyone should experience in these divisive times. Mr. Coombs brilliantly elucidates how we can all hold true to ourselves while still listening to, honoring, and respecting others, even when we disagree. Everyone should read this book!

—Alexander Cendese Actor, Writer, and Producer

We believe what we think. We know we are right. From this place, we treat each other horribly. *The Ruby Rule* presents an option counterintuitive to our prideful ego but psychologically rock solid. Art Coombs consistently invites us to a higher state of civility through awareness, choice, and intentional effort. When you read *The Ruby Rule,* you will find support for all three.

—Paul H. Jenkins, PhD, Positivity Psychologist,
Speaker, and Author

In today's world, it seems no one can disagree peacefully. But with *The Ruby Rule,* Arthur F. Coombs III teaches you how to have honest, productive discussions about opposing views without the argument. The revolutionary Ruby Rule is a step up from the Golden Rule. I firmly believe everyone's communication skills can be improved by learning and applying the Ruby Rule.

—Melissa Dalton Martinez,
Producer and Host of *The Book Break*

Arthur F. Coombs III deftly tackles how to interact with people who have opposing points of view about controversial subjects, including race, cancel culture, politics, and religion by employing *The Ruby Rule.* [This] book is an outstanding call to action and would serve as an excellent launching point for group discussions.

—BlueInk Review

THE
RUBY
RULE

Other Books by Arthur F. Coombs III

Don't Just Manage—Lead!

Human Connection: How the "L" Do We Do That?

The Law of Hard-Easy/Easy-Hard:
A Get-Real Guide for Getting the Life You Want

THE
RUBY
RULE

how more listening and less labeling brings more healing and less hating

ARTHUR F. COOMBS III

Cover design by MiblArt
Interior print design and layout by Marny K. Parkin
Ebook design and layout by Marny K. Parkin
Diamond icon from Freepik.com

Published by Scrivener Books

ISBN 978-1-949165-34-0 (paperback)
ISBN 978-1-949165-35-7 (ebook)
ISBN 978-1-949165-36-4 (hardback)

ACKNOWLEDGMENTS

It would violate everything this book is about for me not to acknowledge a few key individuals who contributed to this writing.

First and foremost, Chris Yates, you are the best writing, collaborating, partnering friend a person could have. I love how well we work together, and your contributions make me so much better than I really am. My humblest gratitude is extended your way.

To Kathy, who helped on book 1, *Don't Just Manage, LEAD!* and now on book four, *The Ruby Rule*. Thanks for your ideas and contributions; they are so valuable.

To my friends at Eschler Editing—I know I can be a pain to work with at times. I am always grateful for your professionalism and patience. I know I am one of many authors you work with, and I am thankful you continue to allow me to do business with you.

To Eric Rescigno, one of my dearest friends. You always seem to be there when I need a laugh. Your foreword is perfect. I am so blessed my high school friend is still a best friend.

DEDICATION

I am acutely aware that most skip the dedication and jump straight to the foreword, introduction, or first chapter. I get it. I, too, have been guilty of flipping those preliminary pages without reading a word. However, with this dedication, I know with complete certainty the one person who should read it will read it.

Barbie, it is so appropriate to dedicate this book to you. It's about being kind, loving, tolerant, and forgiving. These are all virtues I need to improve upon significantly. Many may think I'm biased when I say this (I am); however, I have never met anyone who encompasses the above virtues more than you do.

Perhaps I see these virtues so prominently in you because I see them so lacking in me. Nevertheless, living with you, listening to you, laughing with you, learning with and from you year after year convinces me that you are precisely what your actions profess you to be. You have no guile, and your heart is full of love for all.

Thanks for your support. You will recognize almost all the concepts taught in this book because you are the first person I turn to when I want to bounce an idea around. While we sometimes disagree, I never feel threatened and less-than because you think my opinion is impetuous.

And in case you're wondering, yes, I know at times you think my ideas are impetuous, foolish, rough around the edges, and unrefined, yet you have a gentle, subtle way of nudging me in the right direction without being disparaging or argumentative.

I feel so fortunate to be your husband, partner, and best friend. So this book is dedicated to you. You are brilliant and beautiful, and I would be little to nothing without your companionship. You never complain. You're always calm and consoling. You ask me for nothing and endure my impetuous, teasing temperament.

Fair warning: as you read this book, you'll find a few of those salty cuss words I know make you uncomfortable. *Mea culpa.* Please just skip over those. But even with that, you know that such language is part of me. And I'm so grateful you love and accept me for me.

We are each a unique puzzle—our pieces scattered all over as we try putting them together to become whole. Maybe we can line up those border pieces pretty well, but it's those intricate inner pieces that are hard to figure out. Snaking edges don't seem to fit anywhere. The clues to how the puzzle is all supposed to come together are hard to decipher. It can get confusing and frustrating. Barbie, no matter how scattered my pieces are and how unfinished my image is, you still get me. And best of all, you like my in-process puzzle.

True love is not the butterflies I get in my stomach. No. For me, it's knowing deep down that you will be there no matter what. You see the flawed me and patiently help me try to find and fit those missing pieces.

With all my love . . . and quite a few unfinished pieces,

Art

CONTENTS

FOREWORD   xi

INTRODUCTION   1

Be Civil . . . or Else

CHAPTER 1   15

Advice to My Son on the Day of His Wedding
Or, Live the Ruby Rule

CHAPTER 2   39

Looking at the World Through New Glasses
Or, Wait—Am I the Schmuck Here?

CHAPTER 3   55

Instant Certainty
I Know It's True . . . So Shut Up

CHAPTER 4   77

Cancel
And POOF! You're Gone

CHAPTER 5   97

An Eye for an Eye
*Why Loving Your Enemy Feels Better Than Taking
Sweet Revenge on Them—Even Though You Think Revenge
Would Feel Pretty Sweet*

CHAPTER 6   113

   Ten "Love Your Enemy" Hacks
      Because We Need All the Help We Can Get

CHAPTER 7   139

   Light versus Dark
      Scatter the Darkness with Light

CHAPTER 8   153

   I Found the Ailing Public Square in the Hospital Waiting Room
      A Plea to the Silent Majority to Make Their Voices Heard

CHAPTER 9   167

   Enter the Vault
      Creating a Psychological Safe Place for Civil Discourse

CHAPTER 10   193

   The Mummified Cheerleader, the Trans-Am Dude, and
   Civil Restraint
      How to Practice Mental Jiujitsu

CONCLUSION   223

   Where We've Been, Where We're Going

NOTES   233

NOTE TO THE READER   240

ABOUT THE AUTHOR   241

FOREWORD

by

Eric Rescigno

Author J. D. Salinger said, "What really knocks me out is a book that, when you're all done reading it, you wish the author that wrote it was a terrific friend of yours and you could call him up on the phone whenever you felt like it. That doesn't happen much, though."

I just finished reading a draft of this book, and I definitely feel that way. Fortunately, in this instance, the author *is* my friend and I *can* call him whenever I feel like it.

I have known Art for nearly fifty years. We grew up in Cupertino, California, while the technology boom was in its infancy. Back then, Cupertino was a quaint town in the southwest corner of the Bay Area. Sure, Apple was this little desktop computer company, but nothing like it is today—Cupertino was not the very center of technology and computing that it is today.

We both came from fantastic families, our upbringings like the 1970s family sitcom *Happy Days*. (It would be great if I could tell you that Art and I were like *Happy Days*' iconic, cool, badass Fonzi, but, truth be told, we were more like the uncool but loveably goofy Richie and Potsie).

Art and I did everything together. Football. Classes. Studying. Dances. Double dates. Hanging out. Laughing our butts off. We were just teenagers trying to navigate life the best way we knew how. And more often than not, we did not know how.

We were mischievous and loved to have a good time. We never had any ill will or sought out confrontation. Of course, confrontation sometimes found us.

For example, reading Art's thoughts on the concept of instant certainty reminded me of an experience we had in 1979. We were seniors in high school and were making a Slurpee run to 7-Eleven.

We were in Art's light-blue 1972 Volkswagen Beetle. The funny thing about this car is that it had something called an automatic stick shift. It looked like your standard stick shift except it did not have a clutch. Or, more specifically, it had no clutch pedal.

To shift, you let up on the gas just as you would when shifting a regular standard transmission. This car, however, had an "automatic vacuum pump clutch." When you let up on the gas and softly touched the stick shift, that vacuum pump would engage and you could then shift gears. Today, stick shifts (i.e., manual transmissions) are nearing extinction, but this style of automatic stick shift has been extinct for decades.

In Art's Beetle, the vacuum pump that engaged the gears had a hole in it, and occasionally it would not properly engage. When that happened, the result was the same as trying to shift a normal standard transmission without pressing the clutch pedal: a ghastly gear-grinding noise that got the attention of everyone in the vicinity of the Beetle.

As we were leaving 7-Eleven, sure enough, the Beatle and vacuum pump decided to act up. There we were, trying to merge onto the main road from the convenience-store parking lot, and we were stuck. Art kept trying to engage the clutch, but all he got was the awful sound of metal gears grinding and clanking. The more he tried to shift and go, the louder the noise got. The cars behind us waiting to get out of the parking lot grew more and more impatient. In their eyes, this was a young driver who obviously didn't know how to drive a stick.

The car directly behind us was a jacked-up muscle car with huge rear wheels and a modified scoop on the hood. And the driver inside really put the "muscle" into muscle car. At first, he waited patiently, but soon he became frustrated. As Art frantically tried to get the car to go, the grinding gears seemed to get even louder and more obnoxious, and as I doubled over in laughter, the driver behind us leaned out his window and started shouting, "Push in the clutch!"

After a few more fruitless seconds, he yelled again, louder, "Push in the clutch!" And then again, he screamed at the top of his lungs, "PUUUUUSH IN THE CLUUUUUTCH!"

With this, Art calmly got out of the bug and walked back to the driver.

I stopped laughing.

Is Art going to tell this driver off? I wondered. *Is he going to start something? Am I going to have to hop out and tag team Art in an asphalt wrestling match?*

Art walked up to the guy, who was red-faced and leaning out his window, and coolly said, "I could use your help. Could you show me which pedal is the clutch?" I did not know it at the time, but Art had just used a bit of mental jiujitsu on the frustrated muscly guy (more about mental jiu-jitsu in chapter 10). Asking him to help locate the clutch would allow him to realize that we were not ignorant teens who did not know how to drive a car with a clutch and that he was the one being a bit unreasonable.

The driver, now utterly exasperated, got out of his rumbly muscle car and stomped over to the bug. As he looked into the Beetle, the disgusted look on his face turned to one of puzzlement. Instead of sounding angry, he now sounded surprised. "Hey," he said, "there's no clutch in this car. That's weird, man. How do you shift?"

With that, Art jumped back in, and, like magic, the little bug decided to cooperate. The clutch engaged, and we drove off. I could hardly breathe due to my laughing.

The driver behind us had instant certainty—he just knew—that we were two young drivers who were barely learning to drive a stick. He also had instant certainty that the bug was a normal stick shift and had a clutch pedal. It's important for us to be aware that what we think we know as rock-solid truth might not be.

For example, in my experience as a football coach, I find players, coaches, referees, and fans who can all see the same play but interpret and analyze it from extremely different perspectives. When in doubt about what they see, think, or feel, their brains fill in the gaps based on *their* experiences, expectations, prejudices, and beliefs. This often causes them to perceive or believe something as a fact that is not.

Art dives headlong into this concept of instant certainty in chapter 3.

As my friendship with Art grew, I learned that Art was raised in the Mormon faith. I was brought up Catholic. Through Art, I learned that you could find common ground and good in most religions. But his religious beliefs weren't what really impressed me about Art. It was his character—which was not for sale at any price. His work ethic was unmatched, as was his competitiveness. This very book is a testament to that. Art will be the first to tell you he struggled greatly in school. I know Art, and I know this book is a massive labor of love. He may not show it at first—it's not who he is—but deep down inside, he is a man of faith and loves others. I have seen him do things for others quietly and never seek recognition or praise.

A few years ago, the high school team I coached was going to play one of the top high school teams in Utah. I had no film on this team and was a bit blind as to their strengths and weaknesses. I asked Art to go to one of their games and film it for me. Little did I know the game would be a five-hour drive for him on a Friday afternoon. But Art didn't say anything, and he didn't mind. He took a day off work, and he and his wife filmed the game because it was important to me. This is just one of many examples where I have seen Art live the Ruby Rule.

What is the Ruby Rule? In this book, you will learn all about it. It will help you relate to others in the different relationships you have, especially those you dislike and struggle with.

For me, as a high school football coach, it should be required reading. Art talks about inspiring change in people through emotion or listening to people when it seems like you know all the answers. I can't tell you how often I call a play because I'm the coach and I KNOW it's the right play to call. But then I'll see the kids' eyes and expressions and I can tell they think my play isn't the best. Finally, one of the team leaders will speak up and say, "Coach, I think we should run this play." Like all humans, I'm guilty of instant certainty, too, so I don't always listen to them. I'm the coach, after all. I get paid to lead. I get paid to know what to do. However, when I listen without my ego attached to the decision and run the play they want, it almost always works.

This book will make you laugh, fill you with hope, and mostly make you understand that your relationships are really the most important thing in your life.

As life changes, people tend to come in and out of your life. My closest and dearest friend is my brother Ian, but Art is a close second. Art is always there to make me laugh and see things from a fresh perspective. When you are lucky enough to have a friend like Art, you are lucky enough.

—Eric Rescigno

BE CIVIL . . . OR ELSE

Tired?

Are you tired of the bickering, arguing, and anger you see on social media? I am.

Are you like me and don't know what news station to watch because you want one that is unbiased and calls the news objectively?

It doesn't matter what major news channel I watch; they all seem to report the news with an agenda, like they're trying to convince me of their perspective of the news rather than just reporting the news.

This book isn't about the flaws with news reporting. It's about what polarized news reporting and media are symptomatic of—a deeply polarized nation. It's about the incivility, anger, and unwillingness to listen or compromise we see online and off every day. And it's about how we as individuals can navigate the polarized world, respond to it, and work to defuse it.

The erosion of patience, civility, tolerance, and compassion in our society is a big problem—and it's getting worse. You can't turn on the TV without hearing toxic bickering. News professionals and their guests sling mean-spirited mud at each other while zealous viewers cheer from the anonymity of their sofas and recliners. Okay, I admit I enjoy the spectacle from time to time—the outlandish language and stunts once reserved only for the *Jerry Springer Show*. It can be entertaining. And certainly, as individuals, we might throw up our hands and say, "Yeah, but what can I do about it?"

We see people jump online and engage in blatant cyberbullying, trolling, inflaming, and making nasty comments.

Do you know anyone who has stopped talking with a neighbor because of a yard sign for a candidate on the "dark side"?

If you haven't done any of that, then perhaps you're like me and have indulged in negative thoughts about a friend, family member, or neighbor who espouses a view you find utterly stupid and completely wrong. I think we've all been there.

For our democracy to thrive, we need the freedom to have an opinion and express it. Opposing beliefs are necessary, as is the need to engage with others in public forums. However, today's brazen incivility is shutting us down. Especially moderates. Who wants to enter those mosh pits of incivility and get your moderate teeth metaphorically knocked out? If you feel this way to some degree or another, I'm with you.

When this happens, we wind up with those on the extreme fringes controlling the narrative and driving the discourse. And they won't stop screaming about how the other extreme fringe is completely whacked.

For some time now, the trend toward division has been consistent, with incivility becoming disdain for those with opposing views on key issues. This poisons the well of rational thinking. People stop trying to understand opposing views and listen only to those who agree with them. It makes it an all-or-nothing game where one side is either all right or all wrong.

FACT: No one has a monopoly on truth.

My friends and I do not always see eye to eye, and that is not just okay, it's good. It's healthy. It's democratic.

But what I love about the people I hang with is that we are friends, we are civil, and we respect each other's opposing opinions.

This book is a plea for each of us to be softer, gentler, and kinder. We need increased civility founded in true empathy for one another. And we need it now, more than ever.

This explosion of incivility has fed the growth of disdain for those on the other side. It is this choleric scorn that deeply disturbs me. Before we can enjoy the fruits of healthy civility, we must first suck the poison out of the wounds as we would a rattlesnake bite. We must root out the toxic disdain and hatred that plague our culture.

That sounds like a tall order. You might be reading this and thinking, *I'm just one person. What difference can I possibly make in turning the tide against incivility and anger?*

I often think the same thing. But I will make the case in this book that starting at the individual level is the only way to turn the tide. I'll even outline a few concrete steps and techniques you can implement to help you get started: Small things. Maybe not easy things, but small things that will hopefully begin to make a difference in your life and the lives of those around you.

Disagreement Drives Democracy

This world is full of broad, diverse opinions. These differences make us better. Lively debate is critical to creating optimal outcomes. In fact, in America, civil debate is a constitutional right. You protect your beliefs by protecting others' beliefs, especially when their opinions are contrary to yours.

You not only have the right to respectfully disagree with others, but, in a sense, it's your civic duty. You have no obligation to agree with them. You can believe their policies are terrible, evil perhaps. Or just stupid. But you have a responsibility to disagree respectfully. That is democracy at its core.

The people with whom we differ are human and worthy of decency. Harassing, screaming, mocking, shaming, threatening, intimidating, or using violence is savagery, not civility. It is hate, not love. Long-lasting change happens only when love is the primary motivator.

You have an inalienable right to believe whatever you want. But your right to believe it doesn't imply that whatever you believe *is* right. Let's try more polite passion via talking, debating, listening, and voting whenever possible. And then, when we don't see eye to eye, let's agree to respectfully disagree.

Beyond a Difference of Opinion

I don't want to be overly simplistic. There is a difference between agreeing to disagree and taking a stand against truly harmful beliefs. Many of today's polarizing debates confront harmful beliefs, and it's dangerous and shortsighted to categorize it all as a difference of opinion.

For example, a difference of opinion for me might be disagreeing with a coworker about the best way to reduce air pollution or how tax brackets should work. But if I see through social media that my coworker harbors a truly harmful belief, one that dehumanizes others, like the KKK's stance on race or the Westboro Church's stance on LGBTQIA people, then "agree to disagree" doesn't really apply for me.

How would I go about interacting with that coworker, knowing she's an avid racist?

These are opportunities for productive conversation. Hate, anger, and violence are never the way.

More on that in later chapters—especially the insights offered by Sarah Silverman.

Why Me? Why My Voice? Why This Topic?

After writing my last book, *Hard-Easy*, I was speaking at a conference to a large organization. During the Q&A segment after my presentation, a woman asked me, "How do you write books on topics that have millions of books already written on the topic? Leadership, human connection, self-help—aren't all those topics exhausted?"

I felt there was another question behind her question: *What makes you an expert on this or any topic? Why should I listen to you?*

Here's what I told her:

"I'm offering my thoughts and my opinions. True, they may be on the same topic, but they are based on my unique experiences and insights. For that reason and that reason alone, they are undeniably exclusive by default and valuable. I mean, why should anyone else write novels or poetry anymore? Haven't all topics and themes been written about? Like, a million times over? Why keep making movies? Why keep making music? Why start a new business? I mean, there are a billion businesses today, and there have been a trillion since hominids began trading acorns for grasshoppers. What's the point of another new business?

"I'm hoping that my perspective might benefit a few of the 7.8 billion others wandering this planet trying to figure life out.

"I have no delusions. I'll never be a Brené Brown, Arthur Brooks, or Stephen Covey. But there may be someone out there struggling with challenges I, too, have struggled with. Maybe there is a parent with a dyslexic son. Or there's a student in college who doubts herself and wonders if she even belongs.

"Perhaps there's someone out there who needs to understand the relationship between motivation and habits.

"Maybe a new manager is wrestling with the subtle yet profound differences between leadership and management.

"Maybe there are others who are frustrated with the anger and division they see growing in our society.

"I feel that if I can inspire just one, that one may inspire another. And they may inspire a few more, and so on. True, some dislike my ideas and writing style. That comes with the territory. But if my story moves just one, it is all worthwhile to me—and to that one person as well."

My answer to her is how I feel about this book. We all possess one authoritative something no one in this world possesses: our singularly unique perspective and life experience. Yesterday, you experienced events that created a string of emotions absolutely unique to you and you alone. You're the only one on earth who saw what you saw and experienced what you experienced.

This book is about communicating my ideas, especially those ideas that may be controversial in nature—but spawned in a mind and time unique to one person among the billions alive today and the trillions who have lived since *Homo sapiens* arrived on the scene.

Have we exhausted all possible thoughts, ideas, and stories? No way! Our stories are priceless. We still love to tell them, and, more importantly, there is an audience. We love to listen to others tell them.

Be a Storyteller, but More Importantly, Be a Story Holder

As you continue to read, you will see I like telling stories. But I must tell you that as important as being a storyteller is, it's far more important to be a *story holder.* The most persuasive way to connect with someone is to listen to them. Simply listen. Be a receptacle for another's story.

The most valuable thing we can ever give each other is our loving attention. Loving silence and making someone feel understood has far more power to soften their heart than the most well-intentioned words.

Invite others to share their stories by listening and you become a story holder. The more stories you hold, the more people will share and the more empathy you'll feel for each other.

And I'm not talking about only listening to someone you agree with. That's easy. You already love listening to those folks. Of utmost importance is to be a story holder for those with whom you disagree.

I know birds of a feather flock together and we enjoy associating with others who see the world as we see it. But I submit that you just may find inner peace and contentment as you've never experienced if you soften your heart, open your mind, hang out with, and allow yourself to listen to someone who does not see the world as you see it.

Faulty Altruism

Here is a problematic, illogical line of thinking that underlies the tribalized animosity poisoning our thinking: "My views and beliefs are inspired by love for others and are rational solutions to vexing challenges; therefore, it follows that those who disagree with me are inspired by hate and irrationality."

Ask yourself, Do I feel this way?

If we are honest, many of us do—even if we're not fully aware of it.

Another reason for this book is to inspire some sincere self-evaluation because we all have blind spots and weak-point areas we would be wise to strengthen. But you can't strengthen something if you aren't aware that it's an issue.

So many of us stand around looking at each other, mystified as to why others don't see things the way we do. It's easy to point fingers and blame others. I like to remind myself that it's a shorter path than I think to go from refusing to listen to ideas from those you disagree with to alienation, anger, and hatred.

Guess what? Democracy cannot thrive, and possibly not survive, under conditions of homogenous thought paired with alienated populations unwilling to listen to and constructively debate with those who disagree with them. We need varying opinions, free speech, and the humility to allow for respectful disagreement.

I would also argue that at the microlevel—in our personal lives—to live a rich, full life, we must open our minds and hearts to the perspectives of those who don't agree with us.

I propose that it is an act of love and human kindness to listen to and consider the beliefs of someone we disagree with on various issues.

Remember, real love doesn't have the luxury of picking and choosing who is deserving of its acceptance. Unconditional love is unconditional, even when we disagree.

Stories Backed with Data, Not Data Backed with Stories

When we talk about communicating with love, compassion, and tolerance, we're talking about ideas and concepts people feel in their hearts.

Sure, I could quote study after study and commission survey after survey to intellectually prove and quantify the points I stress in this book. I know a few may find hard facts and facts alone compelling and be swayed by analytical evidence. But I believe most people won't be motivated to change until their hearts are convinced their heads have it right.

Life is not all about data, evidence, and concrete proof. Don't get me wrong—I believe in the power of data-based evidence, the scientific method, statistics, studies, and research. But hard facts, in and of themselves, will change the hearts and behavior of very few.

If you've read my other books, you know I like teaching with stories first and then backing the morals of those stories with some data and references. I believe stories are the most powerful medium when it comes to teaching principles and inspiring change. No one has ever gone the extra mile because of a graph or spreadsheet. They do it based on the emotions they feel.

You can show me study after study, survey after survey, graph after graph, and they're just numbers to me. But when you tell me a story and verbally describe your feelings, I can emotionally go there in some small way. So this book is full of stories, analogies, and metaphors. Some I've borrowed; many come from my life.

I've Got a Long Way to Go

As I reread this book, I am painfully reminded of how imperfect I am and how far I must go in my development as an empathic, supportive, loving human being. I make many mistakes, but I want to try. And I hope that as you read this book, you will double down and try with me.

I hope it encourages you to pause and think, *How can I be just a bit softer? How can I be just a bit gentler and more loving? How can I not rush to judgment?* If even one reader out there embraces this challenge with me, it will be a success.

The Rule Continuum: Golden, Platinum, and Ruby

The concepts in this book are all facets of something I call the Ruby Rule. It is not meant to replace the Golden Rule; it's the ultimate evolutionary end of the Golden Rule. You know the Golden Rule, but you may not know the Platinum Rule, which some have proposed as an extension of the Golden Rule. Both rules have merit, but now I want to introduce you to the Ruby Rule—a level of human civility, interaction, and love that describes a transcendent, inspiring, unmatched way of treating others.

As I introduce you to the Ruby Rule, I'm not meaning to eliminate the other two; each rule applies as determined by social familiarity.

The Golden Rule:
Treat others as _you_ want to be treated.

Pro	Con
If I don't know you or you will not allow me to know you, I should treat you with the principles of the Golden Rule; it is better than no rule at all.	The Golden Rule is not universal; it is situational. If you do not want to be treated the way I want to be treated yet I insist I treat you the way I would like to be treated, things start to break down. Taken to the extreme, it can be a bit narcissistic. The focus is on me, not the person with whom I'm interacting.

The Platinum Rule:
Treat others as *they* want to be treated.

Pro	Con
This rule encourages empathy, connection, and familiarity. For me to treat you how you want to be treated (not how I would want to be treated), I must get to know you. It requires me to reach out and connect with you, see things from your point of view, and act with empathy.	Sometimes, people may want to be treated in harmful or inappropriate ways. For example, my daughter's school starts early. For her to get there on time, she needs to leave by 7:15 a.m. That means she is up by 6:00 a.m. to get ready. She is a notorious late-nighter, and waking early is extremely difficult for her. If I treat her the way she wants to be treated, I let her sleep in and then, every day, call the school and give them an excuse for her being late. This is not in her long-term best interest.

The Ruby Rule:
Treat others to exceed *their* expectations.

> The Ruby Rule uses the pros of both the Golden and Platinum rules and tries to anticipate how to honor both rules while going a little further. The Golden and Platinum rules strive to **meet** one's expectations, but the Ruby Rule strives to **exceed** one's expectations—something that's in harmony with both the Golden and Platinum rules. They are like concentric circles of intensity and impact that emanate from the same philosophical core.

So how do we elevate our altruism from Gold to Platinum and Platinum to Ruby?

We must:

1. Embrace productive, not destructive arguments

2. Change our perspective

3. Avoid instant certainty

4. Resist the cancel-culture movement

5. Oppose the eye-for-an-eye mindset

6. Learn to love our enemies

7. Recognize and embrace light and truth

8. Speak up

9. Create vaulted conversations

10. Use civil restraint to bring about a profound transformation

Each of the following chapters goes is designed to help us all raise our game and change for the better.

Be the Change

"Be the change that you wish to see in the world."

Many people attribute this quote to Gandhi. And why not? It sounds Gandhi-ish. But he never said that.

Here's what he really said:

"We but mirror the world. All the tendencies present in the outer world are to be found in the world of our body. If we could change ourselves, the tendencies in the world would also change. As a man changes his own nature, so does the attitude of the world change towards him. This is the divine mystery supreme. A wonderful thing it is and the source of our happiness. We need not wait to see what others do."[1]

Pretty deep, metaphysical stuff. The abridged version is still great advice, and even though Gandhi never said it, I think he'd back the sentiment. Both statements are relevant to the point of this book.

Change is constant for humans. But not everyone has grasped that for big changes to occur in society, we must initiate change within ourselves. It is impossible to change your external reality without first changing your internal reality. If we start with the goal of changing the world, we fail, but if we start by changing ourselves, the change in the world is natural and inevitable.

If we want to turn hate to love, bigotry to tolerance, bias to equality, and apathy to empathy, we start with ourselves.

Are you ready to go Ruby? Are YOU ready to change? The world is—and it needs you.

Chapter Recap

• The erosion of patience, civility, tolerance, and compassion in our society is a big problem and getting worse.

• Incivility can grow into disdain for those holding opposing views and poisons the well of rational thinking.

• You protect your beliefs by protecting others' beliefs, especially when those beliefs are contrary to yours.

• You have an inalienable right to believe whatever you want, but that doesn't mean—or even imply—that whatever you believe is right.

• We all possess one authoritative something no one in this world has: our singularly unique perspective and life experience. Share that with others.

• When you are comfortable with disdain, it is easy to justify violent words and actions.

• No one is motivated to change until the heart is confident that the head has it right.

- Progress does not stop when we stop talking; progress stops when we stop listening.

- It is impossible to change your external reality without first changing your internal reality.

- Loving someone who does not love you back is a test of *your* character.

- This ability to have an open, honest free exchange of polarized messages without demonizing the messengers with disdain is vital to democracy.

- Your opinions should never undermine or erode compassion.

Pause and Think

- The next time you watch a major TV network, see if you can hear the bias in how the news is presented. Change to a channel that is on the opposite end of the spectrum and listen to their news. See if you can identify the ways they present and reinforce their bias.

- The next time you are angry with someone who thinks differently from you, pause and ask yourself, "Do I feel disdain for the message or the messenger?"

- Have you ever stood up for someone who does not think and believe as you do? What happened, and how did it make you feel?

- How can you be more open with your thoughts and opinions yet maintain grace, respect, and adoration for those who want to tear you down?

- What is more compelling to you—facts or emotions?

- Can you love someone who feels open disdain for you? Is that something you can wrap your head around?

CHAPTER 1

ADVICE TO MY SON ON THE DAY OF HIS WEDDING
Or, Live the Ruby Rule

Perhaps there is no greater petri dish in which to test the resilience of communication and civility than in a marriage or long-term, serious relationship.

I know this well because I am a veteran of the marriage game and have plenty of successes and mistakes under my belt.

So when my son A. J. married his betrothed, Tosh, in the fall of 2020, I had some advice for them—a few nuggets to help them on their hopefully long journey into life together, things that would help them grow closer and more united, navigate the challenges that awaited them, and fall deeper in love year by year.

It might be a surprise to you that I told them to argue more.

Huh?

Bear with me.

Let me set the stage for you.

Our wedding singer, Ryan, was killing it. (Although somebody in my family vetoed my suggestion for "Fat-Bottomed Girls." Godspeed, Freddie Mercury.)

Big windows showed a panorama of mountain peaks and blue sky and allowed sunlight to pour into the room. It was another apt symbol for the wedding: love is like the sun, warming and illuminating those who bask in its light.

Or whatever.

I'm no poet. I was just glad it wasn't raining that day.

In any case, I shared my advice with my son and his bride.

"I love you both," I began.

Good start.

"You are young, good-looking, intelligent, and, like all young newlyweds, blissfully ignorant of the challenges and joy that lay before you. So, this day, I ask you to make me a promise: promise me that you will have at least one argument a day."

Any divorce attorneys reading this will likely be scribbling notes to make some follow-up calls to A. J. and Tosh in the coming months. "An argument a day drives the spouse away," the divorce attorneys say.

In answer to their puzzled expressions, I continued. "You heard me right," I said. "I urge you to dig in your heels and discuss, debate, and disagree at least once a day.

"Now, you may be wondering, *Where is the old man going with this? Did he mean to say that? Did someone spike the punch without his knowledge? Is he having an episode of early-onset dementia? Maybe he's getting a kickback from divorce attorneys if he works this argue-once-a-day thing into his wedding speech.*

"Let me explain," I said.

And that's where I'll pause the speech for now.

Arguing Every Day in Today's World

If your frame of reference for what constitutes an *argument* is what you see in today's polarized political and social discourse, you might be horrified by my advice to the newlyweds.

What constitutes "arguing" in today's world?

The arguments we see today tend to be full of mean-spirited insults, twisted truths or outright lies, vicious trolling, rude interruptions, offensive language and gestures, slurs, and even hate speech. (And you might be thinking about now, *Why would you advise newlyweds to get into* that *every day*? Stay with me.)

Here are a few examples of today's arguments for flavor— though I'm pretty sure you've seen plenty of examples that far exceed these.

(DISCLAIMER: You should know that here and throughout this book, I'll be citing some horrible, offensive, hate-filled quotes and examples. Don't worry; I'll be citing positive, uplifting, and love-filled examples and quotes too. I feel I can't talk about real love without also talking about real hate, so if you're bummed by a negative-energy excerpt, remember, my purpose in using it is to contrast and illuminate the spirit of love, unity, and civility I want this book to promote. So, let's dive in with some negative examples of arguments designed to incite anger, prejudice, and hate.)

Right-Leaning

Rush Limbaugh on African Americans: "They're 12 percent of the population. Who the hell cares?"[2]

Left-Leaning

Twitter user replying to the Republican governor of Arizona, Doug Ducey, on his removing occupant limits on businesses during COVID-19: "I f***ing hate you for this and can't wait to vote you out."[3]

Unhinged-Leaning

Alex Jones talking about eating his liberal neighbors in the apocalypse: "I'm starting to think about having to eat my neighbors. You think I like sizing up my neighbor, how I'm going to haul him up by a chain and chop his a** up? I'll do it. But I'm literally looking at my neighbors now and going I'm ready to hang them up and gut them and skin them and chop them up."[4]

Umm . . .

Yeah. A. J. and Tosh (and all of the rest of you), DO NOT argue like the above examples. And no cannibalism. Cannibalism has been shown to ruin 99.999 percent of marriages.

The problem with this de-evolution in communication and civil discourse is that it is a perversion of the original meaning of the word *argument*.

Many think that the fundamentals of a good argument were developed as two cavemen fought over the last chunk of sloth meat, one caveman bared his teeth and yelled, and the other beat his chest. Then the first one howled and hopped up and down. And finally, the other one clobbered his foe with a club. After taking his opponent out with the club, he probably tweeted about what a lowlife his unconscious rival was. LOL. #WillWakeUpHungry.

And, no doubt, if you assess what constitutes argument today, you might think our caveman scenario is the most likely origin of argument.

Argument, however, was originally formalized in ancient Greece as a method of presenting multiple viewpoints and courses of action. Orators and writers argued for or against policies, laws, and actions.

Who were these orators and writers?

Some were lawmakers and holders of office but also citizens of the city-state.

This fundamental mechanism of democracy was practiced by the ancient Greeks, and it was the duty of every citizen in the democracy to present arguments and judge the merits of others' arguments. The Romans, too, adopted this style of government before they grew into an empire and became a republic (and at times a dictatorship).

The theory was that most people would hear all the arguments presented and choose the option that led to the most benefits for the most people. (I suppose, then, that Greek-style democracy worked at my son's wedding: I made an argument for "Fat-Bottomed Girls" to be sung by the wedding singer, the citizens of our family unit made counterarguments, and based on the merits of each argument, the majority chose the option that led to the most benefits for the most people. I mean, they were obviously wrong, but I was willing to abide by the ruling . . .).

Civility's Role in Argument

Civility is an interesting concept. Let me take you on a brief history of the meaning of civility over the millennia. That's important because civility has not always meant what it means today.

And what does it mean today?

Today, *civility* is defined as formal courtesy and politeness in behavior or speech. Some synonyms are *good manners, deference, courtesy, kindness, consideration, respect,* and *graciousness*.

In an informal poll I took, family and friends described civility as a shared belief of behavioral norms—how individuals ought to act in given situations.

That seems straightforward.

Is it?

Is it civil for a restaurant owner to refuse to serve a patron because the restauranteur disagrees with the patron's opinions on immigration, abortion, and taxes?

I guess your assessment may depend on whether your opinions on those topics align more closely with the restaurant owner (his or her actions promote civility and tolerance for humanity by taking a stand against those who support laws and policies that are intolerant and inhumane) or the patrons (they are victims of incivility, which creates anger, hostility, and division).

Here's another scenario: What if a group of people decides to dump a bunch of tea into a harbor to protest increased taxes on said tea? Who is acting uncivilly? The tea dumpers or tea taxers?

The concept of civility—and its root word, *civitas*—originated in Rome. The citizens there were united by the law that bound them together, giving them responsibilities and the rights of citizenship. In other words, civility originally described being a citizen, obeying the laws of the government, and receiving the protections and privileges of those laws. That's similar to how the Greeks saw it. And entwined in that notion was working together—not too terribly far from our modern notions of civility.

Of course, by the time the Middle Ages rolled around, the meaning of civility morphed. In England, there were royalty and nobles on one side and vassals, serfs, and peasants on the other. Civility defined the ruling class. (Conveniently, the ruling class got to determine what constituted civility.) It was a code of conduct toward other nobles—how to act, speak, and dress. But if the ruling class embodied civility, they considered the vassals, serfs, and peasants uncivil. Barbaric. Barely human. Civility differentiated classes.

This idea carried over into any circumstance where a nation with superior military technology conquered and colonized another land. The conquerors? Civil. The conquered? Barbaric.

The concept of civility is a marker differentiating those in power from those who wield virtually no power. Of course, the "uncivilized" can actually use incivility (according to those in power) as a tool to bring about social or political change. Whether we're talking about the Reformation, the American Revolution, women's suffrage, the equal rights movement, the labor movement, or the civil rights movement, at one time, all were (or still are) deemed uncivil. In that light, I could argue that democracy requires incivility to thrive, endure, and grow.

So where does that leave us?

Well, I suppose there are two different kinds of argument: productive and destructive. *Productive argument* should be the lubricant of society and government, just as the ancient Greeks and Romans intended. It has as its end the greatest good and at its heart compromising with others to arrive at a mutually acceptable course of action.

Destructive argument, on the other hand, pits two sides against each other with the goal of determining a "winner." As such, it has as its end unrelenting resentment, fury, and hatred. At its heart is no compromise, no surrender—even to the detriment and potential destruction of all people and institutions involved.

Civility may be in the eye of the beholder, but I think true civility is linked to principles generally recognized as, or promoting, an improved humanity.

I hope we can agree that Stalin (and dare I suggest Putin) was a brutal dictator consumed with bloodlust and an insatiable appetite for power, King George operated an oppressive regime on his colonists, and the newly minted Americans weren't exactly living by the Golden Rule when it came to the original Americans who had been on the continent long before they were.

And speaking of the Golden Rule, I would now like to tell you how nearly being beaten to death by a giant belt buckle helped me come up with something I now call the Ruby Rule.

Raising the Bar for Civility—The Ruby Rule

It was the spring of 1979, and I was just finishing my senior year of high school. That year, our local church and many similar local congregations participated in what they called a dance festival.

About every five years, thousands of church youth in the region participated in this festival. This year, it was being held on the football field of Foothill College in Los Altos Hills, California. There would be three thousand youth performing for an anticipated crowd of eight thousand. Most of the crowd would be parents, siblings, grandparents, and other extended family members.

I think the dance festival was created to provide an inspirational experience for church teenagers. For me, the rehearsal was a sweltering, sweaty Saturday spent on a football field where we occasionally were called to come out and rehearse our assigned dances and then gather as a massive, collective body at the end to practice the grand finale. I was only there because my parents guilted me into it.

Much of the day was spent with our local youth in an assigned end-zone area where we had set up tents in an informal circle. If we were not on the field being barked at by some lady in the stadium press box whose screechy voice was made even more screechy by the PA system, we were sitting in our tents, trying to escape the heat and sun.

Well, that wasn't the only way to beat the heat.

Our group began to have water-balloon fights. First, it was girls against boys. Then it was our congregation against their congregation. At one point, the adult leaders got in on the fun and it was youth against the leaders.

You could always tell those leaders we liked more than others. They were the wettest, which was kind of a compliment. We chased and drenched the leaders we thought were the coolest (pun intended). And they didn't just lie down and take it. They got us back good.

We loved it.

Then arrived the game-changer. The Goliath. The behemoth. The titan.

A boulder-sized water balloon.

It took several of us to fill the thing. We couldn't even fill it to capacity because it would be too heavy to carry.

I don't know if you've ever tried to carry a water balloon that size, but it's next to impossible. The water shifts, jiggles, and morphs, sloshing from side to side. Three of us struggled to carry it.

But we did.

Once the mega balloon was filled and tied off and we had perfected our mode of carrying it around, the discussion turned to the target. Who among our leaders would get the nuclear balloon?

We decided on Doug Miller, a relatively young (maybe thirty-five), good-natured, and well-liked leader. He always seemed to be up for some fun. And yet, he had not been involved in the water-balloon wars—and therefore was dry.

We dispatched scouts to spot him. The scouts must have blabbed a lot to passersby because somehow word got out that we had a nuclear balloon and that our target was Doug. A rather large crowd started to gather in our area.

Just then, one of our scouts rushed back to report that our target was approaching from the north. The three of us took the balloon and crept to a hiding spot where we could intercept Doug.

To avoid the fate of hurling the balloon at him only to have it bounce off his back and burst on the ground, we planned to sneak up behind him, rest the balloon on his shoulders for a millisecond, then use our fingernails to pop it. Sure, we would get wet, but so would our prey. And we were already wet anyway.

As we silently crouched behind one of the tents, we saw our quarry. He strolled by us, oblivious. The crowd watched in electric anticipation. We slowly got up, managing the Death Balloon with six hands, and tried to move as quickly and quietly as possible.

We executed our plan flawlessly. He never saw us coming, and we got the balloon on his shoulders before popping it. Squploosh!

The water engulfed him.

I laughed. My crew laughed. The large crowd laughed.

Doug Miller did not laugh.

My accomplices and I didn't realize that at first. We, the balloon assassins, scampered away, assuming a massive water balloon fight was about to break out. We needed to find cover.

As I ran away, I cut through the center of our circled tents where the crowd was most dense. But something was off. No one was laughing anymore. In fact, their demeanor had radically changed.

There was an uncomfortable tension in the air. Ominous tension.

As I glanced over my shoulder, I saw Doug striding into the center of our tent area, red-faced and furious.

I remember thinking, *That's weird. He's usually easygoing and just one of the youth.* I wondered why he looked so angry.

My accomplices melted into the crowd. I ran a few more steps and looked back again. Doug was pulling his belt out of his belt loops. At the end of the belt hung a massive brass buckle.

I was really confused. All this was supposed to be fun, and that fun was supposed to lead to more fun: a massive water-balloon fight with one of our favorite adults. But that's not how it was playing out.

"Coombs," Doug said in a very un-Doug-Miller-like voice tinged with rage. "You are gonna GET it now. You can run, but you will not hide forever."

Now he was swinging his belt in large, menacing circles. I could hear it swoosh, swoosh, swooshing and see the sun glint off the enormous brass belt buckle as it cut through the air. Even worse, I could see malevolent intent in the eyes of the belt-swinger.

The crowd was stunned. I was stunned. A little water did not warrant this response. My mind raced. Should I keep running? No, he was right: I had to face him sooner or later.

I turned and waited for him. We were now about thirty feet apart.

Whoosh-whoosh-whoosh.

I held my ground, and he kept coming. I calmly said, "Hey, man, it was just a water balloon," but he was focused on taking his revenge. He had gone Jekyll and Hyde. The friendly, laid-back Doug Miller who got along with all the youth was gone. In his place stood a feral beast quivering with anger and a clear intent to do me harm. He ignored me and closed to fifteen feet.

Ugh.

This has turned into one crappy day.

Reasoning wasn't going to work. I had to try something else.

"Doug, you don't want to do this, man. But if you do, you have one swing. I hope you make it count because if I get my hands on you, you will have no hope."

Even though I didn't want a turn this into a physical confrontation, my adrenaline kicked in. My survival chemicals had me amped up as I saw that belt buckle get closer and closer. I knew if it landed in the right spot, it could cause some real damage.

Physically, I had the ability to back up my threat. I was eighteen and probably in the best shape of my life. I had just finished my high school wrestling career and was preparing to wrestle at college in the fall. I liked my odds.

At that moment, Doug stopped.

His face transformed. He was no longer the feral, aggressive man-beast. Mr. Hyde had left his body, and mild-mannered Dr. Jekyll had returned.

He stopped swinging his belt, and his face sunk.

"Doug, I'm sorry if we hurt you," I said. "It was only a water balloon. We thought you'd think it was fun."

He looked around, took stock of himself, and realized he had just lost it—totally lost it—in front of a large group of teenagers to whom he was supposed to be a mentor. If his anger had happened in a car, we would call it road rage. I guess this was balloon rage.

As he stood there in the middle of the audience that had gathered hoping to see fun and games, he started to cry.

I felt sorry for him and wanted to hug him.

To this day, I do not know why he snapped. We never talked about it. Perhaps he was struggling at work. Perhaps he and his wife had just had a fight. Perhaps the heat was getting to him and he didn't want to be there any more than we did. I don't know. But the Doug Miller I had known for years would not have acted like that around us. Ever.

Except for that moment on that day, he did.

I am reminded of something my father used to say: "Everyone is fighting a battle you know nothing about; be kind."

In retrospect, maybe I was being a punk kid, but I honestly thought we were being kind to Doug. I thought we were practicing the Golden Rule: treating Doug the way we would want to be treated.

And this whole story got me thinking about the Golden Rule—what it meant in practice and if there might be higher echelons of the rule and what that might look like. I started thinking of something I call the Platinum Rule.

As I researched for this book, I discovered I wasn't the only one who had explored this avenue of thought.

I found the earliest mention of the Platinum Rule in a book published in 1988 written by Art Fettig; appropriately, it's titled *Platinum Rule*. Then there was another published in 1998 entitled (you guessed it) *The Platinum Rule* written by Tony Alessandra and Michael O'Connor.

Those books matched my vision for the Platinum Rule. Whereas treating others how you want to be treated is the

Golden Rule, the Platinum Rule postulates that you level up the Golden Rule by treating others how *they* want to be treated.

That was the original concept I wanted to explore in this book—the thing I started to write about. But as I delved into what constituted platinum behavior, I began to observe a type of behavior that seemed to be a level beyond platinum. I call it the Ruby Rule.

I know I'm breaking the metaphor of metallics. But just as the highly valuable ruby stands apart as noticeably different from gold and platinum, so, too, does the behavior that defines the Ruby Rule stand apart as noticeably different from gold and platinum behavior.

That's when the Ruby Rule was born.

I'll make observations about all three rules in this book. And I want to be clear: by proposing Platinum and Ruby rules, I am not saying the Golden Rule is insufficient. Quite the contrary! If everyone in the world diligently and consistently practiced the Golden Rule, the world would be orders of magnitude improved.

Instead, think of each rule as appropriate or optimal to practice based on how well you know the person with whom you're interacting.

How My Giant Water Ballooning Got Me Thinking

I was practicing the Golden Rule with my poor youth leader Doug Miller. In other words, I was treating him the way I wanted to be treated.

However, when I think about the water-balloon incident from *his* perspective, I realize that he may have perceived that my crew and I were making fun of him or even humiliating him—and all in front of hundreds of kids.

Isn't his perspective the more important perspective in this situation? My perspective paled in comparison.

The Golden Rule is a good guideline for social interactions, especially when interacting with strangers or someone we don't know well. You can find versions of it in most religious traditions.[5]

Religion	Doctrine	Source
Zoroastrianism	That nature alone is good which refrains from doing another whatsoever is not good for itself.	Dadisten-i-Dinik, 94:5
Christianity	All things whatsoever ye would that men should do to you, do ye so to them; for this is the law and the prophets.	New Testament Matthew 7:1
Islam	No one of you is a believer until he desires for his brother that which he desires for himself.	Qu'ran Sunnah
Taoism	Regard your neighbor's gain as your gain, and your neighbor's loss as your own loss.	T'ai Shang Kan Yin P'ien
Buddhism	Hurt not others in ways that you yourself would find hurtful.	Udana-Varga 5:1
Judaism	What is hateful to you, do not do to your fellowman. This is the entire Law; all the rest is commentary.	Talmud Shabbat 3id
Hinduism	This is the sum of duty; do naught onto others what you would not have them do unto you.	Mahabharata 5:1517

At the core of the Golden Rule is the assumption that what's good for ME must also be good (pleasing, moral, civil) for YOU. And if not, it *should* be.

While you are attempting to be altruistic, your guidepost for action is actually focused inward, on yourself.

Like I said, this is a great rule if you have virtually no information about the person you'd like to help.

But the better you know someone, the more you should follow the Platinum Rule. Why?

Because everybody is different. What you want done to you may *not* be what your youth leader, spouse, or neighbor wants done to them.

At the core of the Platinum Rule is knowing a person well enough to know what he likes and rendering action based on his preferences. Instead of being focused on yourself, your guidepost here is outward looking.

Now, let's move up a level. At the core of the Ruby Rule is knowing what a person likes and prefers so well we begin to anticipate and render things—big and small—that the person doesn't yet even know she needs or wants.

You can see how each rule set is based on the level of emotional intimacy you have with the person you'd like to serve.

I'll illustrate by talking about birthday celebrations. I hate celebrating my birthday in an attention-seeking sort of way. I have no qualms about getting older, but I really loathe big parties, lots of presents, and a lot of hoopla.

What's more, I hate being at restaurants when they bust out in those silly birthday songs, or cheer, or yell for some patron. All those waiters and waitresses gathering around a table and doing a super loud singy, dancy, clappy, obnoxious tribute upsets the serenity of my meal.

And heaven forbid if someone tries to surprise *me* at a restaurant by secretly letting our waiter know it's my birthday. When the horde of annoying waitstaff surrounds our table, I sit through it in utter pain or perhaps even walk out. I know many think it's fun and festive, but for me, it's absolute torture.

My idea of a great birthday dinner is being with my family or even just my wife and enjoying a quiet atmosphere, good food, and great conversation.

That's me.

But I know for a fact that there are some who treat birthdays as the most important day of the year—a day for a big soiree. They plan for months, making it a very big deal. They revel in the pageantry, attention, and spectacle.

With that context, let's explore how each of the three rules—Golden, Platinum, and Ruby—affects birthday-celebration scenarios.

Happy Birthday!—Golden Rule Version

The Golden Rule helps us if we're dealing with strangers or acquaintances about whom we know little.

So let's say I see a woman on the street wearing a sandwich board that says, "HEY, IT'S MY BIRTHDAY!"

The standard of the Golden Rule is that we treat others how we want to be treated. Well, I already told you how I would love to be treated on my birthday: the more low-key, the better.

So I might ignore the stranger on the street completely because I wouldn't want much attention. Or I might smile and quietly wish the woman a happy birthday as I walk by. At most, I might wait until no one else is observing, approach her, inconspicuously give her a twenty-dollar bill, and say, "Happy birthday from a stranger. It's not much but enough to treat yourself to a little something."

Happy Birthday!—Platinum Rule Version

The Platinum Rule helps if we're dealing with people we know moderately well, such as coworkers, friends, neighbors, teachers, students, and so on. Now we strive to treat those people as *they* would want to be treated—not as *we* want to be treated.

Let's say the woman on the street wearing the HEY, IT'S MY BIRTHDAY! sandwich board is a neighbor from down the street. We're not super close, but we've been to each other's houses for dinner and parties, and we've chatted numerous times at our children's activities (sporting events, school performances and plays, the community pool). I happen to know for a fact that she loves attention on her birthday. She's outgoing and loud (in a good way) and loves a festive ruckus.

Fair enough. I now treat her as she would love to be treated, even though I find it a bit uncomfortable. I'm doing it not for me but to bring her an extra measure of joy on her birthday.

So I pull my car over to the curb next to where she's standing, honk my horn, and shout out the window, "Happy birthday!"

Then I get out and wave at passing cars, pointing to my friend's sign, getting other drivers to honk for her. And maybe I even get a group of passing pedestrians to stop and sing an acapella "Happy Birthday!"

Then I give her a hug, hop back in my car, and off I go . . . to decompress from the uncomfortable feeling of doing something I don't particularly enjoy but also to pat myself on the back for helping a neighbor-friend enjoy her birthday even more.

Happy Birthday!—Ruby Rule Version

The Ruby Rule helps us if we're dealing with someone we know extremely well, such as a spouse, lover, child, parent, sibling, or best friend.

Let's suppose my wife, Barbie, loves big birthday bashes and surprises; she's a real party-aholic. But she also knows I hate that stuff. So she says to me, "Why don't we just go out to my favorite Mexican restaurant and have a quiet dinner for my birthday?"

By the way, that's her living the Platinum Rule, treating me how I'd like to be treated.

"Let's go to dinner," I say, "but afterward, I invited some friends over so we can have cake, ice cream, and a proper party for you."

Touché! I've just counter-Platinumed her.

That's not the end of it. I'm treating her as she wants to be treated, but I'm going to go above and beyond. I'm going to anticipate ways she would like to be treated that she isn't yet aware of.

When we go to the car to drive to the restaurant for dinner, she'll find I've decorated the car with streamers and balloons and written in soap on the windows, "Honk for the b-day girl!"

On our way to the restaurant, strangers honk and wave, putting a smile on Barbie's face.

Then, when we get to the restaurant, I've arranged for a mariachi band to meet us on the curb and play for her as she gets out of the car.

Inside, I've paid the staff to do that stupid happy-birthday song where they all gather around the table and clap, shout, and dance and get everyone around us to look over and sing too. And I've hired one of the waiters to shoot off a confetti bomb over our table . . . before the food comes, of course. Nobody likes confetti floaties in their soup like Barbie does.

Next, I've arranged for my sons to come to the restaurant while we're inside and drive our car home. That's because when Barbie and I leave, the limo I've hired will be waiting for us.

And when we get home, instead of a few friends coming over, I've planned a huge gathering of friends, neighbors, and family to surprise Barbie and give her an amazing (and loud) birthday. As part of the surprise, I fly in the cousin and aunt she hasn't seen in a decade, and they pop out of a giant box I've placed in the foyer.

She loves the whole day. I love the day because she loves it . . . although I must fight back some of my feelings of irritability at enduring what for me is a nightmare of noise, attention, and obnoxiousness.

I've applied the Ruby Rule: treating her how she wants to be treated—and then powering up to the next level. I treat her in a way she isn't even aware she wants to be treated until she experiences it.

This level of interaction requires not only knowing the person you're serving so you can be empathetic, it requires knowing that person so well you can anticipate and exceed their needs, desires, and wishes.

Three Degrees of Altruism

I like to think of these rules as existing on an altruism continuum. The degree to which you know someone determines which rule you should follow.

Another way to visualize it is by thinking of a bonfire. As you get closer to the blazing flames, you pass through concentric circles of intensifying heat. On the outskirts (the less you know about someone), you've got the Golden Rule. It's a great choice. But the next concentric circle you enter is warmer—the

Platinum Rule. Here, you know more about the person you want to serve. And finally, when you get next to the fire, the heat surrounds you. That's metaphorical for thoroughly knowing someone and being able to apply the Ruby Rule for him or her.

When you take the time to sincerely listen (i.e., be a story holder) and try to understand the perspective of the others in any situation, only then can you walk in their shoes and empathetically do what they would want done. Only then can you live the Ruby Rule by performing acts of altruism that anticipate the needs and wants of others—often before they even realize what they want or need.

Now, more than ever, we strive to connect and communicate with others across a variety of social classes, races, ages, sexual orientations, and faiths. The Platinum Rule—and to a greater degree, the Ruby Rule—requires understanding others, their histories, their circumstances, and what really matters to them. The highest levels of altruism demand that when we disagree with someone, we use that as a springboard for further listening and conversation. It's a springboard into argument—argument in its original sense—disagreement and debate that's demanding but not demeaning, uplifting but not obnoxious, constructive but not destructive.

How would trying your best to follow these rules change how you think, act, and alter the dynamics in your relationships with your spouse, children, parents, neighbors, strangers, and those you perceive as enemies?

Think of the civility we could create and inspire if we stepped outside ourselves and focused on what others want and need. Perhaps those who witness this will try to raise the bar too. Living the Ruby Rule can be contagious. You can start a wave of true civility all on your own—a wave that travels far beyond you both in space and time!

And, Now, Back to the Wedding

So it is in the context of all these thoughts on civility and the Ruby Rule that I told my son and his new bride to argue at least once a day.

An argument grounded in, and bounded by, civility. Affording each person the right to make their case. Being courteous in listening to and assessing differing viewpoints. Disagreeing without vitriol or violence. Being willing to meet the party you disagree with in the middle.

Above all, an argument that meets the highest of standards—the Ruby Rule.

I finished with the following advice:

"A. J., you should always be striving to put the interests, happiness, and well-being of Tosh above your own—to anticipate them as you get to know her more deeply. And, Tosh, you should also be striving to place the needs, wants, and joy of A. J. above your wishes and desires. You are trying to grow into the person who sacrifices for the other because your love for each other is so strong.

"So when you have this daily argument, I want you to argue for the happiness of the other. I want you to argue for your spouse's position. A. J., if you are choosing a restaurant, make sure you insist on a restaurant Tosh truly enjoys. Tosh, if you are deciding on a movie, make sure you are arguing to see the movie you know A. J. wants to see as opposed to the movie you want to see.

"Live so that you always feel safest in each other's arms. True love is when the happiness of another is imperative to your own."

And thus ended my advice to the starry-eyed A. J. and Tosh.

Somewhere out there, all the divorce attorneys just tore up A. J. and Tosh's phone number and are hoping this Ruby Rule thing doesn't take off.

Chapter Recap

- There are two different kinds of argument: productive and destructive.

- Civility may be in the eye of the beholder, but true civility can be linked to principles generally recognized as, or promoting, a human good.

- At the core of the Ruby Rule is knowing what a person likes and prefers so well that we begin to anticipate and render things—big and small—the person doesn't yet know they need or want.

- **The Golden Rule: Treat others the way you want to be treated.** We should apply the Golden Rule if we don't know the person with whom we are interacting. If I do not know you, I should treat you the way I want to be treated. Living by this rule with strangers is better than living with no rule at all.

- **The Platinum Rule: Treat others the way they want to be treated.** This requires more knowledge of and empathy for those you are interacting with.

- **The Ruby Rule: Treat others to exceed their expectations.** Treat others altruistically in a manner they do not even know they want to be treated. This rule requires anticipating others' needs and goes beyond how they want to be treated, and in a sense is exactly how you would want to be treated if the roles were reversed.

- The better you know someone, the more you can escalate your degrees of altruism from Gold to Pla tinum to Ruby.

Pause and Think

- Have you ever had a Doug Miller moment? In other words, have you ever tried to treat someone according to the Golden Rule and it didn't work out like you thought it would? Or has someone ever treated you in a way they thought was complimentary, kind, or helpful, but it ended up offending or hurting you in some way? Why? What was the root cause of these misunderstandings?

- During the coming week, keep your eye out for a situation where you can apply the Platinum and/or the Ruby Rule for someone. Record in your journal what happened.

- If you find yourself in a discussion with someone with whom you disagree, try to apply the principles of productive, Greek-and-Roman-style argument: afford each other the right to make your case and be courteous in listening to and assessing differing viewpoints, disagree without vitriol, and be willing to meet the party you disagree with in the middle.

CHAPTER 2

LOOKING AT THE WORLD THROUGH NEW GLASSES

Or, Wait—Am I the Schmuck Here?

I remember when my youngest daughter got her first pair of glasses.

As I drove her to school, she marveled at the clarity of her new perception of the world. "Dad," she said with wonder, "I can see every blade of grass."

And "Dad, I had no idea there were so many leaves on the trees."

And "Dad, I can read that sign from here. I had no idea my eyes were that bad."

She was wide-eyed and excited to see her new world in vivid, living color.

Until my daughter tried on those glasses for the first time, she had no idea her view of the world had been distorted. Her blurry world had been her reality. The world did not change once she got those glasses; her perspective did. With a new perspective based on the ability to process more accurate information, her reality changed.

One of the root causes of incivility is blurred perceptions— and the unwillingness to see the world in any other way than what we're accustomed to. It's like my daughter's eyes before glasses: she couldn't see very well—but she didn't *know* that she couldn't see well. It's one thing to have blurry vision; it's an entirely different thing to refuse to see the eye doctor because you know damn well nothing's wrong with your vision, thank you very much.

You can't enhance your vision if you're unwilling to sit in the exam chair.

This reminds me of an experience I had in a traffic jam. It led to a moment where, like my daughter, I put on a new prescription that changed how I saw the world and made me realize how blurry and distorted my vision had been in the first place.

The Road Warrior

In 2001, Utah was preparing to host the 2002 Winter Olympics in and around Salt Lake City, with construction going on everywhere. That meant a lot of congestion and gridlock. Freeways were more often like slow-moving, scorching parking lots.

Despite the hassles, most in the state looked forward to the result: increased public transportation and expanded freeways. Why? Utah's growth rate then, as now, was high. (Over the past ten years, Utah has had the highest growth rate in the nation (17.6 percent),[6] and the state had been steadily growing twenty years before that.) We desperately needed more lanes.

One day that summer, I was driving toward I-15, the only interstate running north and south in Utah. It was a Saturday at about 2 p.m. It was hot. Sweltering. Satan himself would have moaned.

I got to the on-ramp and merged onto I-15 northbound. Within a minute, the traffic slowed to an agonizing crawl. Then it ground to a complete stop.

A traffic jam on a Saturday? It sucked pretty bad.

This was pre-smartphone days, so I had to turn on the radio and hunt for a traffic report to find out what was going on. It turned out the traffic gods had thrown me (and everyone else trapped on I-15 that day) a double whammy: the Utah Department of Transportation (UDOT) had closed multiple lanes due to construction AND there was a terrible multi-car accident about five miles upstream.

So there we all were. A bunch of cars, bumper-to-bumper, baking in the oven with no relief in sight. Cars—and tempers— were overheating.

Many engaged in the irrational lane-changing game. You know—you're stuck in a jam and since no cars can go forward very fast, you and others decide to move side to side, changing lanes, trying to ditch a slow lane and hit the jackpot by landing in a lane that seems to be moving faster.

But no sooner do you land in a new lane than it slows to a stop and the cars in the lane you just abandoned are now cruising, leaving you behind.

I guess we do it because it makes us feel like we're doing something productive, alleviating the frustration of inching toward our destination. But, ultimately, the change-the-lane game tends to make things worse, not only for the people changing lanes but also for the people they constantly cut in front of. An angry chorus of car horns was accompanied by high blood pressure, screaming, and middle fingers.

I watched all this from the far-right lane, where I had remained since merging from the on-ramp. I shook my head in disgust.

What fools, I thought. *No one can do a darned thing about this, and we should all just chill out.*

That was when I heard someone honking.

Okay, truth be told, it seemed that everyone was honking. But there was something different about the sound of this particular horn that drew my attention to the rearview mirror.

I don't know if this makes any sense, but it sounded like a more urgent honk.

Suddenly I identified the source of the urgent honking: a Bronco-like SUV driving on the shoulder and passing all the cars stuck in the jam. He was illegally using the shoulder as his personal commuter lane.

What a jerk, I thought. Maybe I said it aloud. Who knows? It's entirely possible I was frothing at the mouth, full of righteous fury.

All of us hot, angry drivers were stuck here, hardly moving, but at least we all shared the agony. And here came this schmuck, Mr. I'm-Gonna-Beat-the-System.

As I watched him approach, my indignation grew.

Who does this guy think he is?

It was time to act.

I had to stand up for all of us—we, the miserable citizens civilly (irony here) abiding by the law. No way was this guy going to get away with this act of incivility.

When the Bronco was two cars behind me, I nonchalantly but deliberately pulled my truck onto the shoulder to block him.

I zigged. But to my amazement, he zagged, swerving off the pavement and going off-road into the grass median.

That idiot. What's he thinking? He wants to go Mad Max? I'll give him Mad Max.

I quickly dropped my truck into four-wheel drive and pulled into the dirt to cut him off again, this time not so nonchalantly.

I'm nothing if not a warrior for law-abiding civility.

I wondered how many of my fellow traffic jammers would give me the thumbs up, crack a window and yell accolades, or even ask for my address to send me a fruit basket at Christmas.

I had forced him to stop, and I sat there gloating. Karma had granted me this moment of triumph, helping me to right this wrong and stand up against this brazen act of incivility.

Then I saw in the review mirror that the Bronco guy was now getting out of his vehicle.

Really? He wants to mix it up with me? What the heck is this guy's problem?

As the champion of my fellow traffic jammers, I knew I had their support. They *must* have my back since I had theirs.

So I glanced back at him in the review mirror one more time to make sure he wasn't carrying a weapon. Nope—no gun, knife, bat, crowbar, or chains that I could see. It was just him walking directly toward me. I put my truck in park and hopped out too.

If this now-face-to-face exchange was going to go down, so be it. Karma had already shown herself to be on my side. This would just be the exclamation point of fate facing this guy down—with me as her proxy.

I was amped. Ready to get sideways with this other driver. My pores oozed testosterone.

As I stalked toward my nemesis, I paused.

I was prepared to see a man with a full head of steam, ready to throw haymakers and cuss at me.

Instead, I was walking toward a guy in his early thirties—with tears pouring down his face.

He was not full of rage.

He was racked by emotional pain.

I was confused.

My switch flipped again. In a millisecond, I went from *I'm going to put this guy in his place* to *Oh, my gosh. How can I help this poor dude?*

"Please, help me," he said through his tears.

Off my game now, I sheepishly asked, "Uh, why are you driving on the shoulder?"

"My wife is in the hospital," he said. "She's giving birth, but she's had severe complications. I have to get there as fast as possible."

I will never forget the pain in his voice and etched across his face.

So he wasn't the arrogant, laws-do-not-apply-to-me schmuck I thought he was. He was a scared father who loved his wife and unborn child. My heart went out to him.

Just then, another car pulled off the shoulder and parked behind the Bronco. What a trend we had started.

I glanced toward it and saw that it was a police car.

When the officer got out and walked toward us, I started talking to him rapid-fire. A mile a minute. I wanted to be the advocate for the young father. I didn't want the policeman to give him a ticket for driving on the shoulder. I explained what had happened and that the father needed to get to the hospital at the speed of sound.

The officer acted quickly.

He told us both to get back in our cars. He didn't light up his flashers or unleash the siren, but he did want the Bronco driver to get to the hospital safely. The officer looked at me and said, "Turn on your emergency lights and follow a safe distance behind the Bronco."

Hot diggedy damn! I had just been enlisted as an honorary deputy! Not only had I stopped a great injustice to all who were stuck in the roasting traffic jam on I-15, I had also uncovered the truth behind the Bronco's reckless driving, become his advocate to a law-enforcement officer, and been recognized and recruited as an indispensable part of this policeman's plan. And now, the cherry on top was that I got a police escort out of this infernal traffic jam!

Karma, I love you!

We were off in our convoy of mercy. We got to the hospital in just under fifteen minutes.

As the young father stopped and jumped out of his car, he took a split second to say thank you to the officer and me. The officer calmly cut him off and said, "Go. They need you inside."

Man, I was on top of the world as I stood there in the parking lot and watched the Bronco driver sprint into the hospital. It felt great to have been able to help. It felt even better to be out of the traffic jam. *Art,* I said to myself, *you are one amazing guy.*

I was about to get in my truck and drive off when my cop buddy stopped me and said, "Sir, could I see your driver's license and registration?"

I stared at him for a few seconds before my brain registered what he had said.

We were the dynamic duo who had just finished rescuing a young father in distress. Why did he need my license and registration?

"What for?" I asked.

He told me he had been called to the scene because of me— not the Bronco.

"Someone behind you on the interstate called 911. They described you as a crazy driver in a white pickup having a road-rage meltdown. I am assuming you, sir, are that road-rager."

I was shocked.

I had thought all those other drivers stuck on I-15 were on the same page, that the Bronco zipping by on the shoulder was the crazy driver and that I was in the right for having stepped up to stop him.

Now I realized that at least one driver behind me had seen the situation far differently than I had.

My actions had spoken loud and clear to several people who had witnessed them. I made a few key mistakes when it came to communication and civility—and hopefully they will illustrate how the two concepts are inextricably tied.

First, I couldn't see the situation from anyone else's point of view. That alone affects the empathy one can feel—which makes it easier to communicate (verbally and nonverbally) in an uncivil manner.

Second, I assumed everyone felt the same way I did—or should if they didn't. One feels empowered to act and communicate uncivilly if one feels backed by a mob of those who share the same beliefs and unrighteous indignation. I also assumed, or judged, that the actions of the Bronco communicated it was driven by a rude guy flouting the laws and etiquette of the road.

Third, I may have inadvertently catalyzed a chain reaction of incivility by communicating to others who actually did share my beliefs: "Hey, that guy took matters into his own hands and cut off a shoulder driver. Next time I see someone trying to pass us all on the shoulder, I'll follow that guy's example."

For the next twenty minutes, I tried to explain my perspective of the situation we had been in. And the whole time, in the back of my mind, I felt sheepish for thinking the policeman had wanted me to cover the rear of the motorcade.

Nope. He just wanted me to follow so he could give me a ticket.

Of all the horrible twists of fate.

The officer patiently explained that even though the Bronco was breaking the law by passing everyone on the shoulder, I had no right to pull off the road, jump out of my truck, and confront him. I was breaking the law too.

Dang.

After a long lecture from a very young, very professional, very patient police officer, I was let go with a warning.

Needless to say, nowadays, whenever I see a motorist speeding up the on-ramp to jump ahead of all the other cars calmly trying to merge into traffic, or other drivers speeding or zipping in and out of lanes, or even driving along the shoulder to pass,

I now see these situations through a new lens—like my daughter did when she put on her glasses for the first time and saw the world more clearly than ever.

I definitely don't get irked as much when I'm driving. More often than not, I feel empathy instead of anger.

It seems to me, then, that a prerequisite for being able to resist the temptation of thinking and acting under the influence of incivility and disdain is to see the world through that new pair of glasses—to be able to see the fault in your assumptions and be willing to suspend your judgment of others.

It sounds easy, but looking at the state of civility in the nation and world today, it's obviously not.

But what would it look like if we did see it? Here's one promising example—from the world of politics, no less.

Taking a Stand for Civility

In 2020, Democrat Chris Peterson and Republican Spencer Cox contested each other in an election to become governor of the state of Utah.

This is a time of partisan politics—an era of Twitter rage, name-calling, unfounded accusations, slander, and attack ads. No doubt, each candidate was digging his foxhole, ready for a grinding battle. Voters throughout the state waited expectantly to see the fireworks.

Only, the fireworks didn't happen.

Instead, something extraordinary happened—something so unexpected and shocking everyone in the state, and those in the rest of the nation who were watching, felt their jaws drop in disbelief.

The candidates flipped the script on bitter partisan politics and put nation—and empathy—ahead of party.

They filmed commercials together and announced their intention to campaign against each other with . . . you guessed it . . . civility.

Here is the transcript from one of their commercials:

PETERSON [DEMOCRAT]: I'm Chris Peterson.

COX [REPUBLICAN]: And I'm Spencer Cox.

PETERSON: We are currently in the final days of campaigning against each other to be your next governor.

COX: And while I think you should vote for me—

PETERSON: Yeah, but really you should vote for me.

COX: There are some things we both agree on.

PETERSON: We can debate issues without degrading each other's character.

COX: We can disagree without hating each other.

PETERSON: And win or lose, in Utah, we work together.

COX: So let's show the country that there's a better way.

PETERSON: My name's Chris Peterson.

COX: And I'm Spencer Cox.

TOGETHER: And we approve this message.

#StandUnited[7]

I remember seeing this ad when it aired. It stopped me in my tracks. And I still find myself thinking about it.

This ad stands like a lighthouse in a heavy storm of extremely bitter, angry, polarizing culture wars, its call to action for more polite political discourse cutting through the darkness and warning us away from the rocks that will sink us.

While the candidates agreed to disagree on many issues, civility was not one of them. They expressed humble admiration for one another, and though they had differing political views, they vowed to work together to make Utah a better place to live.

Communication requires far more listening than talking. Words should be used to inform and create, not tear down, no matter how much we may disagree.

Civility demands authentic humility. When that's absent, it's next to impossible to have a productive exchange of opposing ideas.

In the report, "Civility in America 2019: Solutions for Tomorrow," researchers note, "The vast majority of Americans—93%—identify incivility as a problem, with most classifying it as a "major" problem (68%). This disturbing rate has changed little since 2010."[8]

The report further states: "Eight in 10 or more [of those Americans surveyed] point to risks to society as dangerously high; almost nine in 10 respondents identify serious ramifications from incivility, including cyberbullying (89%), harassment, violence and hate crimes (88%, equally), intimidation and threats, intolerance, and people feeling less safe in public places (87%, equally)."[9]

Focus on Civility

Let's return to the story of my daughter and her first pair of glasses. Remember her sense of wonder as she experienced corrected vision for the first time?

Not long after getting her glasses, they broke.

To say she was upset about that is an understatement.

I looked at the broken frames and assured her I could easily fix them. All it would take was a dab of superglue.

Sure enough, I was able to glue the fractured frames together. There was only one problem. I accidentally swiped some glue across one of her lenses and smudged it.

When she put her glasses back on, she was heartbroken. Her perception of the world had changed again.

She yearned to see with the clarity her glasses had given her, but a smudge now tainted her vision. She thought all was lost and she'd have to wait several days before getting replacement glasses. She was very distraught.

Luckily, with a bit of fingernail polish remover and some gentle elbow grease, I restored the clarity of her lens.

Until my daughter tried on those glasses for the first time, she had no idea her view of the world was distorted. Her blurry world was her reality; she didn't know any different. Again, it wasn't the world that changed once she got those glasses but her perspective. Thus, her reality changed with it. What she had once believed about the world around her based on her unknowingly imperfect vision was altered. A new truth emerged from a new way to see the world.

Then, when I smudged her new glasses, she went from a clear reality to blurriness, the contrast stark and disappointing.

She would not rest until her new lenses were clean and gave her the clear vision she had come to enjoy—and expect.

Your perception of others and life in general is totally unique to you. No one will ever have the exact same perception as you do because no two individuals have ever had the exact same life experiences.

Your perception changes over time. Your viewpoint at age fifteen is completely different than the one you will have at age fifty. And if you are lucky, you will learn this VERY important life lesson: your perception does not equal truth.

I had that lesson deeply ingrained into my brain one hot summer day in a traffic jam on I-15 as a Bronco tried to use the shoulder to pass me.

My daughter began learning this lesson when she changed her lens and, thus, her reality.

Many go through life thinking their ideas, judgments, and beliefs concerning people, politics, or religion are the ultimate, 100 percent true—and everyone else can just bag it.

Those who see things that way are wrong and yet simultaneously right. Their perception is their reality. Their truth—though unbeknownst to them, is based on blurry vision. They don't know, and often don't want to know, that their perspective is not everyone else's truth.

Once you have an epiphany and accept that your perception does not always equal truth, amazing things begin to take place in your life.

First, you view circumstances and people with more objectivity. You listen to those who have differing opinions and exchange ideas in a spirit of civility. You're probably less judgmental.

You can practice deep empathy and understand the other person's ideas and beliefs without necessarily embracing them. And who knows? You may move closer to the side you disagree with while moving the person with whom you're engaging in dialogue closer to your opinion.

So what happens when you meet people who are fully cemented in their perception and unwilling to entertain other points of view?

That's okay. People can understand and process situations only through their current perspective. You can only accept the situation as it is without trying to convince them otherwise.

The sooner you realize this, the sooner you stop the Sisyphean nightmare of trying to change people to meet your standards, your expectations, your reality, or your truth.

The way to catalyze change in the world is to change yourself. I'll explore that idea further in another chapter.

Another interesting benefit of being able to see things from another's point of view is that you have the power to change your perception—and thereby your reality. Instead of being a victim of circumstances where you think your perception is formed from the things that have happened to you, you can take true control of your life. One of my favorite sayings is: "You see the world not as it is but rather as you are."[10]

If you don't like how something happened, try changing your perspective of the situation.

The people I like to associate with are those who seem to always see the best in others, who always see the glass half full. They almost always see the good in every situation. They perceive the positives and lessons learned from a failure or bitter disappointment.

If you stay focused on the fact that every challenge you face can help you strengthen some weakness in your character, you're more likely to put on those glasses of clarity.

Challenge and question your current perceptions. Play with different lenses to examine your world from various perspectives—perspectives that might be diametrically opposed to those you hold as correct. In doing so, you will not change reality but will most definitely change your reality and, thus, your life.

I believe—in part because I've experienced it—a beautiful inner serenity will expand within you as you seek to recognize blind spots in your perspective and expand your ability see things from multiple points of view. This inner change will manifest itself in the way you communicate with others.

There can be detail and beauty in everyone and every situation if you are willing to accept the fact that your truth is not always reality and that you can change your lens of perception if you do not like your view. You will be as thrilled as my daughter was when she saw the world anew.

And hopefully, you'll be able to learn this lesson without having to succumb to road rage wherein you prevent a desperate father from getting to his wife and baby in the hospital.

Chapter Recap

- One of the root causes of incivility is a blurred perception—and the unwillingness to see the world in any other way than what we're accustomed to.

- A prerequisite to being able to resist the temptation of thinking and acting under the influence of incivility is to see the world through new lenses, as well as the faults in your assumptions, and be willing to suspend your judgment of others.

- We can debate issues without degrading each others' characters. We can disagree without hating each other.

- Many go through life thinking their ideas, judgments, and beliefs concerning people, politics, or religion are 100 percent true. They don't know, and often don't want to know, that their truth is not everyone else's truth.

- If you do not like your view, change your lens of perception.

Pause and Think

- Have you ever been the schmuck when you thought you were the hero? What was the situation? And at what point did your perception change? How did that make you feel? Did it cause a permanent change in your perceptions, thoughts, and behavior?

- Strike up an in-person or social media conversation with someone who has a belief or beliefs you strongly disagree with. Go into the conversation not with an attitude of confrontation but of learning. Even if the person tries to provoke an argument, stay civil and leave the conversation on a civil note. Journal about the experience.

CHAPTER 3

INSTANT CERTAINTY

I Know It's True . . . So Shut Up

We had the porch pirate on video.

He was a young kid. Maybe fifteen or sixteen. Blond, wavy hair and surfer good looks. Light-gray, baggy hoodie.

Someone in our neighborhood caught this teenage thief of porch packages red-handed on their Ring doorbell camera. The kid strolled up to the neighbor's porch, bent over, picked up a cardboard box that had been delivered to the house, and walked off with it.

When our neighbor saw the video hours later, he hopped on the neighborhood social media group and posted a still frame of the thief, tagged it "Crime," and noted in the header, "Porch thief Saturday night." His message read, "Some blonde-haired teen just stole a pkg off our porch. If you know this person, please contact me."

The message made the rounds like wildfire, and now the eyes of the entire neighborhood were on the lookout for this kid. It was only a matter of time before swift justice was served.

But before we unmask the perpetrator, let's look at a few other examples of instant certainty—and how they turned out.

Instant Certainty

Boyd Matheson, the opinion editor at the *Deseret News*, coined the phrase "instant certainty" to describe a specific phenomenon. Basically, it's when a person makes a quick and uncompromising judgment about a person, group, policy, or situation without further research or reflection. They hold their opinion as the truth—infallible—even when evidence says they are incorrect. In his article, "Instant certainty is the enemy of truth and trust," Matheson says—

> We all have experienced the annoying relative, neighbor, or co-worker who is the master of instant certainty. Regardless of the topic, they have a certain solution, opinion, or position. Their understanding is absolute and their view chiseled in granite—they are right, they know it, and through words, tone, and body language, they expect you to instantly agree with them.
>
> The interesting thing to observe is the moment their "certain" opinion is proven wrong. Rather than retreating or even pausing for a nanosecond of self-reflection, they immediately, with equal passion and zeal as their first instant certainty statement, make a new declaration of what is, in their view, the truth.[11]

In addition to being the enemy of truth and trust, instant certainty is the enemy of civility. And that doesn't apply at the individual level only. As Matheson says, "News and media organizations around the world continually feel the pressure to be the first on a story and to declare, on any issue, the absolute certain, authoritative assessment."[12]

This trend in news coverage and consumption, in turn, amplifies the occurrence of instant certainty at the individual level. For example, we tend to follow only the news and social media narratives we agree with—without much critical analysis of the opinions, news, and content presented. So if your news outlet of choice declares it, then, without a doubt (in your mind, anyway), IT MUST BE THE TRUTH. We are then armed with talking points and a growing sense of animus toward anyone who believes or acts differently than we do.

And many news organizations now cater to whipping the mob into a frothy fury by broadcasting nearly nonstop, one-sided argumentation. Why? Because it helps ratings, which draws advertising dollars.

'Tis a vicious, not virtuous, cycle.

But for now, let's hit pause and go back to the porch pirate. Our neighborhood of vigilant vigilantes and their electronic-surveillance eyes were recording everything on and around their property. They were going to get this punk kid if was the last thing they did.

Get Him!

Nothing spreads information as fast as social media, and, sure enough, as soon as my neighbor posted images of the blond teen thief who walked off with a package, neighbors saw it, shared it, and began posting information about this young thug. Apparently, the kid was a budding, enterprising crime kingpin in our neighborhood, our own less-swarthy El Chapo. Here is some of the chatter from the neighbors. Don't worry, this is all true; I cannot make this stuff up:

Neighbor 1: Alert—He and his friends were on bikes.

Neighbor 2: Post on FB [FaceBook] and he will be found.

Neighbor 3: Um, he looks familiar . . . as in I've seen him in other videos before. I don't know who he is though.

Neighbor 4: This guy's clothes look awfully similar to the day-light car break-in nearby.

Neighbor 5: Looks like he's still in high school. Neighbor kids might know him. He looks young.

Neighbor 6: He's probably the same kid who stole 2 mountain bikes on the cul-de-sac within the past two months.

Neighbor 7: My daughter goes to the high school. I have her yearbook now. I'm going through and crosschecking the doorbell image against all the blonde males. I'll private message you a list of potential suspects.

Neighbor 8: Anybody know the new family that moved in a few weeks ago on Pine Avenue? Don't they have a blonde, high-school aged son? Not sayin' it's him, but you never know.

The messages went on and on, boiling into a frenzy based on the certainty that they were right. And my neighbor, victim of the porch pirate, had incontrovertible proof that he had been the target of a crime. He had the scoundrel right there on video. The neighbor couldn't wait for the neighborhood sleuths to expose the thief. He even notified the police, who were sending an officer out to log a report.

Clearly, everyone thought it was an open-and-shut case. (Cue the *Law and Order* gavel sound.)

I App-Solutely Know This Is the Guy Who Started the Fire

There is a crime-tracking and neighborhood-watch app called Citizen. And it's actually a pretty cool concept. Released in 2016 under the name Vigilante, Citizen is heavily used in about twenty large cities.

The app uses police-scanner data and reports as well as video footage from users to create a map of nearby crimes and police responses.

It is a very well-intentioned app—a digitized neighborhood watch that allows you to crowdsource the fight against crime.

But what happens when you throw instant certainty into the mix?

We found out on May 15, 2021.

CEO Andrew Frame was certain he had found the man who started a devastating wildfire near Los Angeles. Citizen users had reported a tip on the arsonist, posting a photo of the suspected fire-starter. Frame was determined that his app would be integral in catching the man.[13]

Frame encouraged his staff to rapidly publish the man's photo, and as soon as it became known, his name.

Frame's crime-fighting gusto caused him to violate his own company's terms of service, which prohibit "posting of specific information that could identify parties involved in an incident." One employee even complained about the violation but was ignored.[14]

Frame messaged his staff: "First name? What is it?! Publish ALL info. FIND THIS F***ER. LET'S GET THIS GUY BEFORE MIDNIGHT HE'S GOING DOWN."[15]

A steady stream of information about the man believed to be the arsonist was published on the Citizen platform. The app even offered a cash reward for information that led to the capture of the alleged arsonist. The amount of the reward offered by Citizen escalated as the hours passed and the man had not been caught.

Frame was all in on his premise that the tip provided by one of his service's users was reliable and true. In that spirit, he continued messaging his staff to inspire fast work and collaboration with the app users to catch the bad guy: "BREAKING NEWS. this guy is the devil. get him. by midnight!@#! we hate this guy. GET HIM."[16]

Note the abundance of ALL CAPS to shout the urgency of the matter.

In any case, Mr. Frame had a solid plan. Except for one glitch.

And it was a colossally big glitch.

Turns out they had identified the wrong person.

Now eight hundred thousand vigilante Californians[17] were out to get an innocent man. And who knows what might have happened had they found him?

Fortunately, the police found and detained the misidentified man before the posse of self-deputized citizens did. The police arrested and charged someone else and released the innocent man.

I know for me, when I fall into instant certainty, I find that it subverts patience, methodical gathering of evidence, critical analysis of facts, and rational thought.

Let's look at a few more examples.

Can We Put These Parents in Time-Out?

In July 2020, about four months into the pandemic, a rather large group of anti-mask parents packed into a courthouse in Utah County to protest a state mandate for public schools. The state legislature would be requiring all K–12 students to wear face coverings to school.

A video of the courtroom shows the place is standing room only, packed shoulder-to-shoulder, and only a few of those in attendance can be seen wearing masks.

The county commission members sat in a semicircle at the raised desk area in front. All but one wore masks in accordance with policy for state and county government buildings and advice from state medical experts.

The county commissioner, Tanner Ainge, announced that it would be a short meeting. Why? He began to explain:[18] "I think this is the exact opposite of what we need to be doing. We are supposed to be physically distancing, wearing masks—"[19]

Before he could finish his sentence, civil discourse disintegrated. A few in the crowd started booing, and others joined in, like fans at a professional wrestling event. Their shouts and boos drowned out Ainge, and he paused a few times before almost shouting into the microphone to be heard.

Bear in mind, this was in a government building. In a courthouse.

You remember courthouses, right? We've known them as places where parties with opposing beliefs get to take turns making arguments before judges and juries in an orderly, civilized manner so that facts can be heard and verdicts rendered.

No matter where you stand on mask policies for K–12 students (this could just as well have been a group of pro-mask parents angrily demanding a mask policy), perhaps we can agree that a mosh pit of disgruntled parents shouting over everyone else and refusing to engage in conversation is less than ideal.

I guess it could have been worse. These parents might have taken out bear and pepper spray, attacked security guards with flagpoles and fire extinguishers, chased the commissioners while calling them traitors and vowing to see them hanged for treason, and rampaged through the building destroying, defacing, and stealing property as they went.

But, hey, something like that would NEVER be perpetuated by U.S. citizens on the institutions of a free democracy. That's just crazy talk.

Ahem.

In any case, back to our story.

In this county commission meeting, as parents booed and shouted down the county commissioner, he continued. "All of our medical experts, our Department of Health—everyone is encouraging us to do that [wear masks and socially distance]. This room is not complying with these health guidelines. This creates a great health concern for this meeting, so I'm going to suspend the rules, and I'm going to make a motion to continue this entire meeting on another date."[20]

More booing and yelling—which had to be spreading micro-particles of saliva all over everyone and into the air. Had I been the county commissioner, I wouldn't have wanted to spend the next hour in that sealed petri dish of contagion either.

Meeting adjourned.

The reality is that this pandemic was unprecedented—at least in anyone's living memory. Many have read about the Spanish flu, which swept across the globe in the early twentieth century nearly one hundred years before COVID-19, killing an estimated five hundred million people worldwide. But no one alive today *lived* through that. In our lifetime, COVID-19 is our first pandemic.

As COVID-19 spread—and especially at the time of the howling parents at the Utah County Commission meeting—we had no conclusive evidence to guide us through this mess and tell us exactly what we should and should not do. Yet, I was fascinated by the instant certainty everyone had on all sorts of coronavirus issues.

Some swore by masks; others said they didn't matter. Then we had some so-called specialists who suggested we wear two masks. Some said the mask must be made of one material, and others that. Some claimed a face shield was more effective; others said no way. Some said outdoor interaction with others was better than indoor. Some said it didn't matter. Some said we should stay six feet apart and others three, and still others said no, it should be ten. Some said we should not have any contact at all, while others said we could bump fists or elbows.

More than two years into the pandemic, things aren't much better. Some currently believe you are stone-cold stupid for NOT getting a vaccine, and others are equally convinced that vaxxers are dumb sheep following blindly. Some say we should still wear masks after being vaccinated, and others say you can go maskless. And then there's the issue of those who have been vaccinated and still get the virus—or those who are infected two or more times.

Like the parents in the county commission meeting, many are passionate that their perspective on the situation is the absolute truth. They have instant certainty because they've heard an expert on the late-night news, read an article in the local newspaper, or seen a post on their social media feed from someone they trust. They now know for sure what is right and what is wrong concerning the pandemic.

It's fine to have a belief, but it seems to me that it's problematic when instant certainty causes someone to refuse to listen to other opinions, self-reflect, critically and objectively evaluate all evidence, feel hostility toward anyone who disagrees with a held belief, and verbally or physically attack those with whom their opinion differs.

The Plane Truth

It's happened so often now it's not all that surprising when we see another story about it. I'm not talking about a Kardashian in the news. No, I'm talking about passenger rage on airplanes. And during the pandemic, a subset of that was mask rage. I'll describe just one example emblematic of many such episodes we saw during the COVID days.

A plane in Utah was on its way to Arizona. The passengers had boarded, and the flight attendants were moving through the cabin to make sure everything was ready to move away from the gate and begin taxiing to the runway.

One man, whom we'll call Jeff, was wearing a face shield and claimed that was enough. Since Jeff believed he was following the airline's policy, he argued with the flight attendant, who asked him to please put on a mask.

In this case, the airline had a policy that passengers had to agree to before the flight. In order to fly on one of their planes, a passenger had to "wear a face covering over [his or her] mouth and nose at all times while traveling."

So Jeff felt instant certainty that he was right. Technically, his mouth and nose were covered by the face shield. The flight attendant, on the other hand, had instant certainty that Jeff was in the wrong, claiming the staff had distributed masks to passengers as they boarded to ensure that everyone had a mask to wear.

Regardless of how you feel about mask-wearing, businesses have the right to establish policies their patrons must follow while using their services, facilities, and vehicles. If a restaurant has a NO ARMADILLOS policy and I ask to be seated while I hold my pet armadillo (I would name him Malcolm), the restaurant will likely refuse to seat me and ask me to leave. What if I sneak Malcolm into the restaurant in a backpack and let him out after I start eating my meal? Especially if other patrons complain, the restaurant will likely kick me and Malcolm out of the restaurant for violating their policy. It's their legal right to do so.

Flash-forward to Jeff's return flight from Arizona to Utah. Oddly enough, he had the same flight attendant. This time, Jeff had a mask covering his mouth but not his nose, and he had a face shield on over the mask. The flight attendant approached Jeff and his wife and said, "Sir and ma'am, I know who you are. You are to keep your mask above your nose at all times." Apparently, on the flight from Utah to Arizona, Jeff and this flight attendant had already gotten into it. So you can see both were prepped and ready to do battle.

Jeff wore the mask the flight attendant had provided him during the previous flight, and he wore the face shield over the mask. But while his mouth was covered, his nose was exposed.

Jeff had instant certainty that because his shield covered his nose, his mask did not have to. The flight attendant informed Jeff that he would not be allowed to fly if he did not comply with the airline's policies, which included that the mask cover his nose.

The airline can uphold its policy in whatever way it deems fit. The way I see it, it's like visiting someone's house, and they ask you to take your shoes off at the door. You may not believe it's necessary to take off your shoes, you may even get anxiety about taking off your shoes, and you may prefer to keep them on. But as a guest, you are polite and willing to follow the rules and policies of the person in whose home you are a guest.

Let me digress for a moment so you can appreciate how the three rules work. If you aren't very familiar with the host who's asked you to remove your shoes, you may opt for the Golden Rule: treat her how you want to be treated. Let's assume you're really irked that you've been asked to take off your shoes. So you take them off, but then in a few minutes, you tell the host you forgot something in your car. When you go out to the car, of course, you must put your shoes on. And when you come back in, you conveniently "forget" to take them off. Why? Because this is how *you* would want to be treated: shoes on.

Perhaps you do know the person pretty well, and you know she is obsessive about keeping a clean house. The Platinum Rule play here would be to treat the guest as *she* wants to be treated. Before she even asks, you've slipped off your shoes and commented on how perfect the house looks.

And if you are a concentric circle closer to knowing her very well, you may go Ruby Rule: anticipate and act in ways the host isn't even aware she wants to be treated. Maybe you know that the root reason the host keeps the house immaculate is an allergy to dust. You call the other guests ahead of time to give them a heads-up about the issue and time to mentally prep if they are anti shoe-removal. And when you show up at the house, you've brought with you Japanese-style indoor slippers, a pair for everyone, so that the host feels less stress, senses your empathy, and feels validated. She's not the only one affected—the guests who may have issues with taking off their shoes feel they have been taken care of.

Here's the point: if you politely ask me to take off my shoes at your house and I don't believe I need to take off my shoes, I typically won't start arguing with you, make rude comments about your shoe beliefs, refuse to take off my shoes, stomp around on your carpet in my shoes, cuss everyone out, and behave in other confrontational ways.

Let's get back to our airline passenger. Jeff could have just said to the flight attendant, "Okay," and adjusted his mask. That would have been the end of it.

Jeff, however, fueled by his instant certainty and frustration, refused to listen to or consider others' beliefs and fears. He argued that the policy's wording was unclear by not specifically listing the word *mask* as a requirement. It's easy to see how unclear communication can result in huge misunderstandings.

Eventually, the passenger sitting in front of Jeff joined the argument and began yelling at him, distressed that Jeff wasn't taking full safety precautions. Ironically, this distressed passenger was also not wearing his mask properly at the time because his mask didn't cover his nose—which, of course, was the initial problem between Jeff and the flight attendant. This escalated emotions for everyone involved.

The flight attendant informed Jeff he would not be able to take this flight. The man in front of Jeff asked him to exit the plane so they could depart. According to witnesses, Jeff, in a not-so-Ruby way, replied, "Mind your own f***ing business." The passenger in front responded by grabbing Jeff, and fisticuffs ensued between the two. Others on the flight jumped into the fray.

Soon, flight attendants and an airline supervisor came to escort Jeff off the plane. As Jeff grabbed his backpack, he reportedly elbowed the passenger in the row in front of him as he exited his row. Another scuffle broke out between Jeff and that passenger. Once again, other passengers jumped in, some to break up the fight and others to land a few blows of their own. An off-duty police officer on the plane intervened, broke up the melee, and escorted Jeff off the plane, where police met him and charged him with disorderly conduct.

Instant certainty and lack of clear communication were the culprits for a lot of the issues in this story.

Jeff instantly *knew* he was being treated unfairly, *knew* he didn't need to wear a mask, *knew* the airline policy was unclear, *knew* the lack of clarity justified his defiance of it, *knew* the passenger in front of him should not have gotten involved, and *knew* the other passenger was, therefore, a bigger problem.

The flight attendant *knew* Jeff was trouble after having a talk with him on their first flight together. Maybe the flight attendant had had a bad day and dealt with other passengers who'd given her a hard time. Her fuse may have been a bit short. To be fair, this flight attendant was simply doing her job, while Jeff was in clear violation of airline policy and refusing to remedy the situation.

The passenger in front of Jeff had instant certainty that Jeff was a jerk refusing to comply with policy. This passenger instantly *knew* Jeff was putting others at risk (like the passenger's mother, who was in hospice), and he *knew* screaming was the best way to communicate how upset he was.

Jeff had many opportunities to stop the confrontation. Had he just complied with the airline's mask policy and not argued, the flight would have taken off, Jeff would have landed in Utah, and all would have been good. Or when Jeff was told about the mask mandate and how to properly wear his mask but didn't want to, he could have voluntarily gotten up and said, "In that case, let me deplane; I will find another way home." No fight, no police citation, no nothing. But Jeff chose neither of these options. He chose to be verbally and physically belligerent.

This is where the Platinum and Ruby rules can help. Treat others how they want to be treated—and try, if you can, to anticipate ways to go above and beyond for someone.

This entire situation could have been avoided had EVERYONE practiced these two complementary rules. If Jeff had followed the Ruby path, he would not have argued with the flight attendant about a policy that was not hers to change, he would have complied immediately, and he would not have been involved in a fight with another passenger. In fact, he would have anticipated that mask policies might cause confusion, approached the flight attendant, and, in a friendly manner, said something like, "I'm still getting used to this mask thing. I know I've gotten it wrong on other flights. But I want to make your job easier. Can you tell me if I'm wearing it right? If not, I'll fix it."

I think we're beginning to see a pattern with instant certainty and how it erodes civility.

Pie Crimes and Misdemeanors

One summer day, when I was about fourteen years old, my mother was in the kitchen making lemon-meringue pies.

When she was done, she put the pies in the refrigerator to keep them cool. Unusual as it was, all six of us kids were in the house that afternoon.

At one point, from wherever we were in the house, we all heard my mother shriek. That was startling. The next utterance from her sent shivers of dread into the heart of each child. She called us each by name, clearly summoning us because one or all of us were in trouble for something.

"Cary, Linda, Art, Kay, and Mike, come down to this living room this instant."

My youngest sister was about four and thus exempt from the coming wrath.

As we all gathered in the living room, we exchanged looks and whispered to each other, "What did you do?" to which each of us responded, "I didn't do anything. What did *you* do?"

Like a seasoned interrogator, Mom ratcheted up the tension by letting us sit there for a few minutes before she walked into the living room.

Then she entered the room, sat in a chair facing us, and emotionally said, "I have been slaving away on those pies all morning. I was going to give them to people who have shown kindness to our family. However, I just opened the refrigerator, and one of the pies has a large slice missing."

Gulp. I felt bad for whoever stole a slice of Mom's pie. Be that as it may, I was glad I wasn't the one about to be sent to the pie gulag.

"I want you to be honest," she said to us. "Tell me if you were the one who took it without asking me."

She then stared at each of us one by one—a very Clint Eastwood moment.

We all just sat there and shifted in our seats, silently willing the guilty pie thief to step forward. But no one did.

As we sat there in silence, my older sister said, "Come on, guys. Please, whoever did it, confess so those of us that are innocent can get back to what we were doing. I have tons of things I need to get done."

Again, nerve-racking silence. None of us looked at my mom.

Mom said, "Okay, if that's the way you want it." She stood up and declared her verdict. "None of you are leaving until the guilty party confesses."

We all groaned. We all had great afternoons and evenings planned. We all shared our plans with Mom at once, hoping she would see how cruel it was to ruin the day for four innocent kids just to punish the one guilty kid.

"But I was going to watch my favorite show."

"I was going to go play with friends outside."

"I was supposed to meet a friend at the mall."

"I wanted to go swimming."

"Pleaaaaase? I've got so much to do today!"

Mom listened and then replied, "As soon as the one who ate the pie steps forward, everyone else can go about their business. But until then, you are staying exactly where you are."

We groaned in unison. "But, Mom, this isn't fair. You can't do this."

"I *can* do this," she said. "It's already done. No one else is here in the house, and I know it was one of you that ate the piece of pie. No one is leaving until that person confesses."

Mom left the room. I'm sure she figured we would soon turn on each other like rabid dogs.

Which we did.

As we looked at each other, we started pleading. My older sister said, "Please, if you ate the pie, say so. This isn't fair to everyone else. It's okay. None of us will be mad at you. Just confess and let the rest of us all have a great day."

No one said anything. The pie thief stayed quiet. It was like a real-life game of Clue, and we had to figure out who did it before we could be set free. We debated, cajoled, threatened, and pled.

The more we debated, the more adamant each of us was that he or she was not the guilty party. Time ticked by. The longer we sat, the angrier and more frustrated we got with each other. We even started lobbing accusations.

Finally, one of my sisters said, "Okay, I didn't do it, but I'll confess so that we can all get out of here. The punishment Mom must have in store can't be worse than this. But know this: if I find out who really ate it, I'll be coming for you."

Aha! She was clearly the pie bandit. Why else was she willing to confess? I wasn't buying the altruism angle. She *had* to be the pie eater. So this confession she was trying to spin into the selfless act of throwing herself on the sword was bogus. But I didn't really care. If she wanted to confess, and I could go to the pool with my friends, more power to her.

By this point, an hour had passed.

Just then, my father came home. As he walked into the entryway, he stopped and looked at us sitting there. We all had long, sad faces, and he could tell something bad had gone down.

Mom walked in. Dad could tell she was in a foul mood, cocked and ready to fire, so he chose his words carefully. In an even-keeled tone, he asked, "Honey, why are all the kids sitting in the living room looking so sad?"

Mom was ready to get my dad in on this attempt to coerce a confession. "I made lemon meringue pies this morning," she said. "I had planned to give them to some of the neighbors, but this afternoon, when I went to the refrigerator, one of the pies had a big piece missing. I know one of the kids ate it, but I don't know who. The one who did it won't confess, and if any of the other kids know who it was, they're not telling, so they all have to sit there until the guilty party comes forward."

Dad got a really weird look on his face. It was a mixture of surprise, humor—and dread.

Mom looked irritably at him, angry perhaps that he wasn't immediately raging into the living room to demand a confession.

He cleared his throat, and with a measured, soft cadence, he said, "Honey, I came home for a quick lunch this afternoon. I thought you had made the pies for the family. I was the one who took the slice. Then I had to rush back to the office. I guess you didn't know I had come home. It was only for a few minutes. I'm sorry."

Upon hearing this, Mom burst into tears.

We kids all quietly got up and went back to the things we had been planning to do.

Later, Mom apologized to each of us for her instant certainty. She had jumped to conclusions and wrongfully accused us. (I'm glad there was no Citizen app back then. I'd hate to have a vigilante mob after us innocent kids accused of burgling a slice of pie.)

Years later, whenever the topic came up, Dad smiled and said with a teasing wink, "That was the best lemon meringue pie I've ever had."

It was definitely not funny at the time—other than to my dad, that is. But this will always be one of our family's folklore stories. My mom had instant certainty that one of us kids had eaten her pie. I had instant certainty that my sister, who was going to confess just to get us out of time-out, was indeed the pie bandit. My father had instant certainty that the pie his wife had made was for our family (he loved pies).

You know, one thing I've learned in business is that it's invaluable for a leader to admit, "I simply don't know. I have a hunch that x is happening, and y is what we should do to respond. But I have no conclusive data to support that theory."

Saying you are not exactly sure is something a leader does if they want to instill trust in those they lead. It also helps you steer clear of the pitfalls of instant certainty.

The other thing leaders should do is admit when they are wrong. When you are presented with facts—cold, hard, indisputable facts—that prove to you and the rest of the world that your early assumptions on any given topic were wrong, for your credibility, it's critical to step up and admit you were wrong. As we have seen, this is tremendously difficult for those afflicted with instant certainty.

My mother admitted she was wrong about her instant certainty that one of us kids had eaten her meringue pie. She gathered us together, and with tears in her eyes, admitted her fault. She'd jumped to conclusions and made all of us kids suffer, and she felt terrible. She felt terrible for forcing us to sit there for so long. She felt terrible for encouraging us to turn on each other. She felt horrible about not trusting us. She was in real pain, her apology touched our hearts, and we all felt bad. She even let us choose a favorite meal she would prepare. I remember my mother humbly asking us for forgiveness. That powerful lesson has stayed with me.

Can you imagine what would have happened if the instantly certain president of one party were to have humbly admitted in various situations, "I don't know" or "Hey, I got it wrong on this one"? Or how about if the instantly certain senator or congressperson of the opposing party uttered those words? Can you imagine the trust that would be built between leaders and constituents? Or would the constituents, afflicted with instant certainty, turn on those leaders? In business, this frank approach builds trust, which enhances relationships, which leads to higher performance and stronger results.

The Porch Pirate Revealed!

Well, you've been patiently waiting for the end of this crime drama. Considering the chapter's topic, however, you may have already guessed the outcome.

You remember my neighbor. He turned to social media and even the police after seeing the doorbell footage of a young blond kid carrying a package away from his porch. Well, he posted a sheepish update for the neighborhood social media group. The mystery was solved:

> False alarm. My sister sent my nephew to grab the package off the porch and put it into our garage, as we are out of town. I did not know he was going to do that and did not recognize him on the video. Sister confirmed it was him. Sorry to waste anyone's time. Now I have to cancel a police report.

Before he issued his update, his instant certainty infected his neighbors. Suddenly, they were certain this kid was the perpetrator of other crimes in the neighborhood. Every neighbor in the social media group was on high alert for young, blond, teenage boys roaming the area. This neighborhood, like much of Utah, is packed with young, blond, teenage boys. I wonder if all the innocent kids being eyed suspiciously by the neighbors could feel the surveillance.

What's the remedy for instant certainty?

In his article on instant certainty, Matheson concludes:

I have figured out that my instant certainty never ends well and usually undermines whatever trust exists in the relationship. Instant certainty also relegates my understanding to backward-facing thoughts and emotions rather than being open to new truths that can only be found in future-facing discussions.

I have found that checking my instant certainty at the door does wonders to foster more constructive conversations and, not so amazingly, takes me to ideas, opinions and truth I never had supposed.

Embracing uncertainty requires real humility and courageous vulnerability. Being able to say, "I don't know," or "tell me more" or even "I hadn't considered that" builds trust and leads to a more complete view of the truth.

Suspending judgment not only provides space for truth to be discovered, it is actually the only path that leads to learning, understanding and trust. When large institutions, governments, businesses and individual leaders can lay aside their certainty, public trust increases. Perhaps instant uncertainty would lead us to more truth and greater trust.[21]

Amen to that. It's a very Ruby perspective.

Chapter Recap

*   Instant certainty is the enemy of truth, trust, and civility.
*   Many believe passionately that their perspective on a situation is the absolute truth. They have instant certainty because they heard an expert on the late-night news, read an article in the local newspaper, or saw a post on their social media

feed from someone they trusted and now know for sure what is right and what is wrong.

- In business as well as in my personal life, I find that when you admit you are wrong, you build bridges of trust.

- The cure for instant certainty is humility and vulnerability— and the Ruby Rule.

- Make these phrases regulars in your vocabulary: "I don't know"; "Tell me more"; "I hadn't considered that."

Pause and Think

- Think of someone in your life who has instant certainty about something and can't be convinced otherwise—even in the face of evidence to the contrary. How does that affect your interactions with that person?

- Think back to a situation where you initially had a strong, impulsive opinion only to be given more information later that radically changed your judgment. How did this perspective about-face feel once you saw and understood the situation with a 360-degree view?

- Make a goal to bring these phrases into the next conversation you have with someone with whom you disagree: "I hadn't considered that; tell me more."

CHAPTER 4

CANCEL

And POOF! You're Gone

I t was November 2018. The topic of civility had been brewing in my brain for a while, even back then. I published a post on Instagram. The last few sentences sum up the main idea of the post:

> Recognize and accept the fact that your view is not always reality. Starting with "I'm right, and you are wrong" will fuel anger, misunderstanding, and disconnection. Accepting and respecting our differences will foster peace, compromise, and connection. Instead of starting with, "I'm right, and you are wrong," let's try to start with, "I know we are different, and it is not just OK, it's good."

Not bad, right? It's a message promoting unity, overcoming divisiveness, and respecting the differing opinions of others. You don't have to agree with another's opposing point of view; just look beyond the opinion to the human behind it.

Now, let's fast-forward three years.

I received a message from the Instagram content administrator. I figured that maybe the administrator was inspired by one of my posts and wanted to share the love with me.

Nope.

Here's essentially what the message said, "You're canceled."

Cancel Culture

Do you live in the United States, and have you heard the phrase "cancel culture"?

If so, you are part of the 44 percent of Americans who have heard "at least a fair amount" about it.[22]

If not, you land in the cohort of the 56 percent of Americans who say they've heard "nothing or not too much about it."[23]

Today, the term has evolved to mean ostracizing someone who has said or done something offensive or controversial.

Did you know, though, that the term originated in a 1981 disco/funk song, "Your Love Is Cancelled," by the band Chic? It was a term used to describe breaking up with someone. The phrase later made it into the 1991 film *New Jack City*, where it had a more ominous tone, referring to a more permanent breakup: a murder ordered by the leader of a drug cartel. As it turned out, the scriptwriter who made it part of the dialogue was inspired to include it because he happened to be listening to that same Chic song, "Your Love Is Cancelled," as he wrote the scene.[24]

Canceling someone became more of a thing with the advent of social media, which has the power to rally thousands—even millions—of voices to a cause.

Initially, it gave voice to those who normally didn't have a voice against more powerful entities—people and organizations with greater influence, money, and platforms.

The #MeToo movement allowed victims to not feel isolated, alone, and afraid that no one would believe them or listen to them. It gave them strength to know there were victims like them and the courage to share their experiences so that others might escape the same fate.

#BringBackOurGirls in 2014 brought worldwide attention to the terrorist group Boko Haram kidnapping 276 female students from a secondary school in Chibok, Nigeria. The hashtag was retweeted two million times, and it resulted in the rescue of fifty-seven schoolgirls within a few months and the escape or rescue of 102 more girls over the next six years.[25] Not all the girls have found freedom, but we can surmise that because of the hashtag, more girls have been freed than would have been had the campaign not generated so much attention.

However, the mobilization of opinions on social media has been appropriated by others for a variety of purposes. In some cases, it's to act against someone with whose opinion you disagree. In some cases, it's to rabble-rouse. In other cases, it's to enforce perceived social mores. In this sense, cancel culture is merely an incarnation of something that has existed in human civilization since the beginning—the need to scapegoat, pillory, or affix scarlet letters to those who have broken actual laws or merely societal norms and cultural strictures.

Journalist Ligaya Mishan describes the new form of the ancient practice:

The speed, sloppiness and relative anonymity of social media haven't created a radically new strain of bullying; they just facilitate and exacerbate an old one. And some would argue that it's not bullying at all, but the opposite: a means to combat abusive behavior and exploitation of power, and a necessary corrective to the failure of the state to protect its citizens.[26]

Instagram Partially Silences Me

So, back to my Instagram post. If you'll remember, I was advocating for people to not judge each other, to not think they're always right and that the opposition is always wrong, and to listen to others' points of view while respecting the humans expressing those views.

Instagram informed me that it was deleting my post. It was a concise, cryptic, one-sentence message that said my post was too controversial.

I was stunned. I felt violated. It really felt like someone had come into my home and robbed me.

At the time Instagram notified me, I didn't even really remember the post. I had posted it nearly *three years* earlier.

I had to go back through my own website, where I had also posted the message, to find out what I had written to set off this controversy. When I found it, I laughed at the irony of this particular message getting canceled. I was perplexed and angry.

When I contacted Instagram support (which was a herculean feat in and of itself), they were rather dismissive and unwilling to give me any real answers as to how this post about fostering better communication, empathy, and dialogue was controversial. After many attempts, the only answer anyone could give me was that Instagram had several complaints from viewers saying they were offended.

Apparently, my message about "accepting and respecting our differences" was too radical or threatening to some and so they silenced my message. Did the social media platform even bother to read my "offensive" message before erasing it?

Let me pause here to say that Instagram is a business. It can set its own rules. I have no problem with that. They can delete what they want and not have to explain themselves to anyone.

However, my experience with a single Instagram post highlights a point about cancel culture: just because one group says you are wrong, they are not necessarily right.

We live in a world where a few can silence any voice or any opinion they deem offensive—even if the offensive thing isn't an action but a nonaction. I give you exhibit A: Chris Pratt.

Vengeance on an Avenger

Actor Chris Pratt plays the character Star-Lord in *Guardians of the Galaxy* in the Marvel Universe. He's also starred in other movies and TV shows.

In October 2020, some of Pratt's fellow stars in The Avengers franchise participated in a fundraiser for then-presidential candidate Joe Biden. People who made donations to the campaign could then virtually hang out with six of the movies' stars. Pratt, however, did not participate in this event.

Even though Pratt had not declared support for either candidate, he "was blasted on the social media platform by people who said his conspicuous absence was evidence of his secret support of President Donald Trump. From there, the conversation devolved into criticism of Pratt's Christian faith and the church he attends."[27]

To his credit, Pratt did not engage in Twitter fights with the mob. And, unlike fellow actor Gina Carano, he didn't lose his job.

Former MMA fighter Carano is an outspoken conservative who was fired from her role on *The Mandalorian*. She had been sparking Twitter rage for some time. "She issued contentious tweets, one in which she mocked mask-wearing amid the novel coronavirus pandemic and another in which she falsely suggested voter fraud occurred during the 2020 presidential election."[28]

Granted, the straw that broke her employment contract's back was not the wisest thing to say in public: she claimed that "being Republican today is like being Jewish during the Holocaust."[29]

Unlike Pratt's nonaction provocation, here, Carano said something not in good taste—and something definitely insensitive and offensive to many.

That said, it was her opinion. Does that merit her getting fired?

Some thought so. The hashtag #FireGinaCarano started trending.[30]

She was fired. And not only did she lose her current job, she lost lucrative future work in the *Star Wars* franchise:

> Carano's Cara Dune became an instant fan favorite, with the actor praised for bringing a calm strength to the role. But her tweets have also made her a controversial figure among Star Wars fandom. According to sources, Lucasfilm planned to unveil Carano as the star of her own Disney+ series during a December investor's day presentation but scrapped those plans following her November tweets. Multiple Mandalorian spinoffs are in the works from executive producers Jon Favreau and Dave Filoni, including Rangers of the New Republic, which could have potentially starred Carano.[31]

Here's an interesting idea. What if those in the rabid #FireGinaCarano movement had taken the advice of TV's Mr. Rogers (in chapter 9, we'll take a deep dive into his testimony before the U.S. Congress, from which the following quote is taken) and "stopped the mad" they felt? What if they'd quelled their anger and asked themselves, "That's an extreme comparison she's making, and I think it's kind of ignorant and not too well thought out . . . but what is at the root of her statement? How does she feel being a conservative in an industry noted for its liberal-leaning tendencies? How does she feel trying to express her opinion and getting attacked for it? Is there a way we can start a conversation with her on that topic, see where we get, and at least listen to each other?"

And don't for one second think the Twitter mob is made up of only liberals coming after conservatives. It goes both ways with equal nastiness.

Here's a Tweet from a conservative attacking not just liberals but conservatives who aren't conservative enough for this Tweeter. Be warned: this social media troll uses a profusion of offensive obscenities (in some spots, I've used asterisks to make the harsher language a little less so). I'm quoting verbatim here, so you'll see some spelling and grammatical mistakes. I'll leave them as is, just so you get the full flavor of the Tweet.

I believe [Senator Mitt] Romney has been defeated in this war and has switched to the side of the enemy and has become a p***y ass ass face!!

Side note: We know this Tweeter is serious because "p***y ass face" is not enough to express his contempt; he must double up on the "ass."

I think he is a coward with no balls whatsoever. I think he needs to have his ass kicked while America watches.

Side note: Incidentally, I'm not sure what religion this Tweeter is, but many U.S. conservatives are Christian. If this commenter is Christian, then he is certainly quoting from the New Testament here. You know, that famous saying by Jesus where he tells the woman caught in adultery, "I think you need to have your ass kicked while Judea watches." I digress.

Trump on the other hand is a bad a** mother***er he has stuck to his principles he has lived his whole life he has lifted us up and givin us a reminder of what having the unbreakable American spirit can and will do!!! The spirit our founding fathers showed us by standing up to England and kicking their greedy asses back in the day!! as for me I choose to live by those same principles found in our constitution and Declaration of Independence and I will die before any traitor or tyrant try to convince me meantally emotionally spiritually or physically. I'm a conservative I'm a capitalist I am a free man!! to anyone even flirting with liberals, socialists, or communists I say f*ck you and get the f*ck out of my country.

Side note: I suspect many Native Americans are harboring the same "get the f*ck out of my country" sentiments toward Caucasians that this Tweeter expresses toward liberals.

If you want that shit go find a country already practicing it but I will no longer tolerate the disrespect of you soul eating f*ckers any longer it is time for all freedom loving people to draw the line push these aholes out witch means in our day to day activities that if your liberal whiny slimy pathetic mooching ass crosses paths I will not hesitate to put you in your piece of sh*t utopian soulless demonic place no doubt about it!!!

I don't want to poke too much fun at this person. The sad reality is that if we were to have a civil conversation, I know there would be many things he and I would agree on. What I deplore is his way of communicating. If this is how we are going to communicate with each other, humanity is doomed. At the same time, I will defend his right to communicate the way he wants. So I find myself in a conundrum. I want to defend his free speech, but I want to inspire him and others like him to communicate with others in a Ruby Rule sorta way.

This Tweeter spoke with reverence of America's Founding Fathers. Perhaps he forgot the concepts of *e pluribus unum*: out of many, one; and "united we stand, divided we fall." Or that the Constitution was born in debates where people who disagreed deeply engaged in civil discourse and made key compromises to create that foundational document for a new experiment in freedom.

In any case, there is no civility in the molten rage behind the canceling and bullying and attacking taking place in our country today.

I see two key reasons why this manner of discourse (e.g., canceling, bullying, attacking) is dangerous for a civil, democratic society: 1) it subverts the constitutional principle of due process, and 2) it silences the potentially calming, balancing voice of moderates who are afraid to become a lightning rod for harassment, canceling, and rage from those who disagree with them.

Canceling, Scapegoats, and Due Process

The idea of the scapegoat—a person, object, or entity blamed for the wrongs of others—originated with an actual goat. The Old Testament book of Leviticus (chapter 16) describes a ritual wherein the Jewish chief priest takes a goat and symbolically lays upon it the sins of all the tribes of Israel before banishing the goat to the wilderness, the goat taking with it all the sins of the people. It gave the Israelites a clean slate, so to speak.

The ancient Greeks and other civilizations designated an actual person to be banished in atonement for the maladies and misdeeds of the people. Sometimes, instead of banishment, a civilization opted for human sacrifice of the scapegoat. (Nine out of ten actual goats surveyed preferred this method.)

Scapegoating as a form of cancelation has existed in one form or another since humans began forming tribes and holding raves in caves. McCarthyism in the United States during the 1950s sought to cancel artists and entertainers conservatives didn't like. They accomplished this under the guise of "quelling Communism."

In May 2021, Alexander Lukashenko, despicable dictator of Belarus at the time of this writing, sent his military jets to force an Irish airliner to land so he could kidnap a young journalist and Belarusian opposition leader Roman Protasevich and his girlfriend, Sophia Sapega. Protasevich is paying for his dissent—and the dissent of other Belarusian protesters and freedom activists—by being sent to Lukashenko's torture prison.

There have always been attempts to cancel or destroy those perceived as enemies.

One big problem with the current version of canceling empowered by social media is that it is a form of vigilante justice. As you know, vigilantes may actually end up putting some criminals out of commission. (Yay!) But, as has happened in real life too many times, vigilantes also mistakenly target innocent people. (Boo!)

In Mexico, an uncle and nephew, ages forty-three and twenty-one, were in the central part of Acatlán to buy construction supplies to finish a well they were building. A few locals started accosting them. Apparently, a rumor being spread via

WhatsApp asked the citizens of Acatlán to be on the lookout for child kidnappers on the loose:

> Please everyone be alert because a plague of child kidnappers has entered the country. It appears that these criminals are involved in organ trafficking. . . . In the past few days, children aged four, eight and 14 have disappeared and some of these kids have been found dead with signs that their organs were removed. Their abdomens had been cut open and were empty.[32]

Some citizens assumed when they saw these two men, whom they didn't recognize, near an elementary school that they were the kidnappers. They confronted the men angrily. More people joined the crowd. Some texted or called for more people to come and help: the kidnappers had been found!

Police took the two men into custody—not because they thought they were kidnappers but to protect them from the growing mob.

The mob followed the police car, eventually broke into the police station, dragged the two men out, and murdered them.

Meanwhile, in India:

> Twenty-seven people have been killed in 13 incidents of vigilante attacks inspired by false WhatsApp messages warning of child kidnappers or organ harvesters since May. Many of the attacks have targeted strangers in remote communities, including people from another region or who speak a different language from the mob.[33]

Of course, due process isn't perfect either. With the advances in DNA testing and genealogical databases, more and more people who have been sentenced to death or long terms for violent crimes are being found innocent and released, some after spending three, four, or even five decades behind bars for crimes they didn't commit. But the system initially let them down.

Still, at least with the imperfect system, there is a chance for someone to receive due process and not be mauled by the mob. As it guarantees in the U.S. Constitution: "No person shall . . . be deprived of life, liberty, or property, without due process of law" (Fifth Amendment), and "nor shall any State deprive any person of life, liberty, or property, without due process of law" (Section One of the Fourteenth Amendment).

How many of our canceled or attacked (via social media) fellow humans get due process from the social media mob? That's a problem.

Baseless and unproven claims, rumors, and lies fan the flames of fury that undermine humanity and lead to innocent people getting shamed, hurt, and losing their jobs, friends, and dignity. And in the most extreme instances, they can lose their lives, as we saw in the stories from Mexico and India. And lest you think the United States is immune from such horrific mix-ups, there's the story of Kolby Marquise Graham in Dallas, Texas. He was shot in the head by Norman Christopher Collier IV, 22, who "believed false rumors spread on social media regarding his brother's killer, and then shot and killed an innocent man."[34]

The Silenced Majority

I believe many in the political middle have grown fearful of expressing their opinions because the fringes are so loud, extreme, and angry that they dare not speak up for fear of being shouted down.

Bari Weiss discusses this phenomenon in her article, "The Self-Silencing Majority." Weiss was an editor and writer at the

Wall Street Journal from 2013 to 2017 and then at the *New York Times* from 2017 to 2020. She famously resigned from the *New York Times* in 2020.

In her resignation letter, she wrote:

> But the lessons that ought to have followed the [2020 presidential] election—lessons about the importance of understanding other Americans, the necessity of resisting tribalism, and the centrality of the free exchange of ideas to a democratic society—have not been learned. Instead, a new consensus has emerged in the press, but perhaps especially at this paper: that truth isn't a process of collective discovery, but an orthodoxy already known to an enlightened few whose job is to inform everyone else.[35]

After her very public resignation, Weiss heard from "a lot of people who live in fear of saying what they really think. In red America and in blue America—and, perhaps more so, on the red internet and the blue internet." She describes this as "an epidemic of self-silencing."[36]

For the moderates who fear the Left, Weiss writes:

> They are feminists who believe there are biological differences between men and women. Journalists who believe their job is to tell the truth about the world, even when it's inconvenient. Doctors whose only creed is science. Lawyers who will not compromise on the principle of equal treatment under the law. Professors who seek the freedom to write and research without fear of being smeared. In short, they are centrists, libertarians, liberals and progressives who do not ascribe to every single aspect of the new far-left orthodoxy.

As for the moderates who fear the Right, Weiss wrote they find that: "[Freedom of thought and expression] is under siege on the right by the rapid spread of internet cults and conspiracy theories. One need look no further than Rep. Majorie Taylor Greene, an unabashed QAnon believer elected to Congress."

Weiss wistfully longs for the America where

the consensus view relied on a few foundational truths that seemed as obvious as the blue of the sky: the belief that every-one is created in the image of God; the belief that everyone is equal because of it; the presumption of innocence; a revul-sion to mob justice; a commitment to pluralism and free speech, and to liberty of thought and of faith.

As I've observed elsewhere, this worldview recognized that there were whole realms of human life located out-side the province of politics, like friendships, art, music, family and love. It was possible for Supreme Court jus-tices Antonin Scalia and Ruth Bader Ginsburg to be the best of friends, because, as Scalia once said, some things are more important than votes.

Alas, Weiss notes, cancel culture has reduced America to a place where "persuasion is replaced with public shaming. Forgiveness is replaced with punishment. Mercy is replaced with vengeance. Pluralism with conformity; debate with de-platforming; facts with feelings; ideas with identity."

This is what prevents our moderates from entering the fray. Moderate citizens are much like many of the journalists Weiss knows—afraid to speak out because it can turn out bad.

For journalists, Weiss writes:

All this bodes ill, especially for independent-minded young writers and editors paying close attention to what they'll have to do to advance in their careers. Rule One: Speak your mind at your own peril. Rule Two: Never risk commissioning a story that goes against the narrative. Rule Three: Never believe an editor or publisher who urges you to go against the grain. Eventually, the publisher will cave to the mob, the editor will get fired or reassigned, and you'll be hung out to dry.[37]

For average citizens speaking out on social media, she writes:

Thus, it should come as no surprise that a recent national study from the Cato Institute found that 62% of Americans say they self-censor. The more conservative a group is, the more likely they are to hide their views: 52% of Democrats confess to self-censoring compared with 77% of Republicans. And of course they are afraid. In an era when people are smeared for petty things, small grievances and differences of opinion in a supposedly liberal and tolerant environment, who would dare share.[38]

This leads me back to where I began in this chapter: Instagram. I had dared to share a message of unity, tolerance, and civility—and earned the ire of the mob.

A Fleeting Win for the Nonsilent Majority

I fear we are hurtling toward an Orwellian nightmare where words and opinions are banned and history is dismantled. Every day, middle-of-the-road citizens are reluctant to discuss tricky, hard-to-solve social problems.

Maybe I offended some born-again conservative Christians with my Instagram post. Perhaps I offended a group of liberal atheists. Who knows? I never got the real story from Instagram.

I'm guessing the people I spoke with did not know the whole story either.

It is far easier to strike out, scream at, belittle, and try to cancel those you disagree with from the anonymity of your bedroom while sitting in your underwear, hidden behind your profile. The root of canceling someone is all about shaming them. Just because you have an opinion that is politically or socially out of step at the moment shouldn't mean you lose your ability to earn a living; it should not cost you your reputation.

Cancel culture is really not all that different from the past totalitarian regimes and censorship we have seen throughout history. It does not matter if your argument has merit. You say the wrong thing, do the wrong thing, or believe the wrong thing, and you are silenced. You are canceled and made irrelevant.

Our democracy depends on the public square. As Voltaire said, "Think for yourself and let others enjoy the privilege of doing so, too."

When the public square is constrained, we no longer have a free society or effective republic.

Just for reference, here are some examples of constitutionally guaranteed free speech and banned speech.

Freedom of speech includes the right:

Not to speak (specifically, the right not to salute the flag)

> *West Virginia Board of Education v. Barnette*, 319 U.S. 624 (1943)

For students to wear black armbands to school to protest a war ("Students do not shed their constitutional rights at the schoolhouse gate.")

> *Tinker v. Des Moines*, 393 U.S. 503 (1969)

To use certain offensive words and phrases to convey political messages

Cohen v. California, 403 U.S. 15 (1971)

To contribute money (under certain circumstances) to political campaigns

> *Buckley v. Valeo*, 424 U.S. 1 (1976)

To advertise commercial products and professional services (with some restrictions)

> *Virginia Board of Pharmacy v. Virginia Consumer Council*, 425 U.S. 748 (1976); *Bates v. State Bar of Arizona*, 433 U.S. 350 (1977)

To engage in symbolic speech, (e.g., burning the flag in protest)

> *Texas v. Johnson*, 491 U.S. 397 (1989); *United States v. Eichman*, 496 U.S. 310 (1990)

Freedom of speech does not include the right:

To incite actions that would harm others (e.g., "[S]hout[ing] 'fire' in a crowded theater.")

> *Schenck v. United States*, 249 U.S. 47 (1919)

To make or distribute obscene materials

> *Roth v. United States*, 354 U.S. 476 (1957)

To burn draft cards as an anti-war protest

> *United States v. O'Brien*, 391 U.S. 367 (1968)

To permit students to print articles in a school newspaper over the objections of the school administration

> *Hazelwood School District v. Kuhlmeier*, 484 U.S. 260 (1988)

Of students to make an obscene speech at a school-sponsored event

> *Bethel School District #43 v. Fraser*, 478 U.S. 675 (1986)

Of students to advocate illegal drug use at a school-sponsored event

Morse v. Frederick, __ U.S. __ (2007)[39]

Hey, I don't think my post falls anywhere near the naughty free-speech list. In fact, I believe this list vindicates my post. As you can tell, I still have bad feelings regarding this issue. I need to let it go. Or should I let it go?

Maybe that is, in part, what this book is about. Maybe there are too many people like me who just say, "Let it go" and never speak up. If we never speak up, we are canceling ourselves. That is not my style! Ultimately, it's up to every one of us, every reader of this book, every citizen of this country who values the Constitution and the nation born from it. It is up to us to take individual steps, even if they're small, toward defanging cancel culture.

So, what do we do to help stem the tide of cancel culture?

First, we arm ourselves with facts. Actual facts. Not something your Uncle Ezra sent you on Facebook posing as a fact. Evidence and facts will help us ignore the emotional tirades and stay calm.

Second, we all must stand up for others when we see them being attacked and criticized, even when we do not totally agree with them. I have seen this done on my social media sites, and it is incredible how trolls will scamper back to their holes when just one person steps up and says, "I don't think that's what Art meant." Or "I think your comment is unwarranted." It gives me room and space to jump in and try to calm the situation down.

Apparently, Voltaire was anti-cancel culture too: "It is clear that the individual who persecutes a man, his brother, because he is not of the same opinion, is a monster."[40] We need to call out those who are being mobbish, troll-like, cancel-culture monsters.

Third, we need to do something that may sound simple but proves to be exceptionally difficult at times: agree to disagree in a way that's civil.

The only way to keep free speech is to exercise free speech. If you choose not to speak up, you may, in time, lose that ability to speak up.

Cancel culture has a long and dark history. It undermines the very principles our freedom is built on.

I am sure some will be offended by the opinions I offer in this book and will try to cancel the book and me. If encouraging others to "foster peace, compromise, and connection" is a bad thing, then let them try. I, for one, will be practicing my First Amendment right and will speak my mind—and I will civilly engage with those who civilly engage with me, even if we disagree.

I hope more people do the same and meet me in the public square for a free exchange of ideas. Let's find that common ground. I know it's there.

And as for Instagram, score one for the silent majority—me—who didn't stay silent. Instagram finally un-canceled me and reposted my message.

Chapter Recap

- Cancel culture and canceling via social media is merely a reincarnation of bullying, scapegoating, mob attack, and censorship.

- To flourish, democracy needs not only freedom of speech but its citizens to participate in the free exchange of ideas.

- To help stem the tide of cancel culture, we must arm ourselves with facts, stand up for others when we see them being attacked and criticized—even when we do not totally agree with them—and reestablish and fight for the social contract of our republic: to agree to disagree in a way that's civil.

- The only way to keep free speech free is to exercise free speech. If you choose not to speak up, you may, in time, lose that ability to speak up.

Pause and Think

- Have you ever been a troll? Joined a mob of like-minded people to attack someone on social media who had a different opinion than yours? In hindsight, would you have behaved differently? Can you think of more positive ways to express yourself?

- Have you ever been the victim of a cancelation attempt? How did it make you feel? Did you do anything about it?

- Have you ever been the moderate peacemaker who jumped in to defend someone against the howling mob and vicious troll attacks? If so, how did it make you feel? In what ways can you think of inspiring others to do the same thing?

CHAPTER 5

AN EYE FOR AN EYE

Why Loving Your Enemy Feels Better Than Taking Sweet Revenge on Them—Even though You Think Revenge Would Feel Pretty Sweet

So far we've been talking about the feelings of irritation and anger caused by focusing on our differences (in politics, religion, social policies, gender, orientation, and class, among others), which can lead to negative thoughts that sometimes spill over into uncivil words and actions.

Incivility, left unchecked, can lead to darker places. It may seem like a big leap to go from exploring uncivil feelings and words to looking at examples of violence—but it's not. I'll provide two examples that illustrate the point.

In the first, I'll simply remind you of "Jeff," the airplane passenger whose tale was told in the previous chapter. I won't delve into it much further; however, it's interesting to note that these were ordinary people doing ordinary things. Misperceptions and misunderstandings led to incivility. Snippy words were exchanged between Jeff and the flight attendant, all based on assumptions or on simply having a rotten day.

Snippy talk escalated quickly to frustration felt by all parties: Jeff, the flight attendant, and, unbeknownst to them, the gentleman sitting in front of Jeff. Frustration quickly escalated to anger manifested by aggressive posturing and yelling. And from there it swelled to a violent altercation: slaps and punches.

These were not bad people who set foot on the plane, looking to pick a fight and punch someone. These were normal people with good intentions whose incivility catalyzed the rapid escalation from thoughts to words to violence in seconds.

And that's the point. It's not a stretch for a normal, everyday, well-intentioned person to get triggered and escalate to physical violence. On the airplane, we're talking about slaps and a punch or two before the parties were physically restrained. "It's just a slap," you may be thinking. However, what if people hadn't been there to intervene? How much further would they have gone? In the news, we read about bar fights that begin with an annoyance or frustration and end with someone punching someone, not intending to kill them, but the punch causes a fatal brain hemorrhage.

And sometimes those fights cause people to *want* to kill someone. Road rage and random altercations put people mentally over the edge, and suddenly you're a rabid, animalistic beast.

Could never happen to me, you might think.

And that's what everyone thinks until it happens to them.

My second example is of a high-profile actor who snapped. In a very public venue. I'm talking about Will Smith slapping comedian and emcee Chris Rock at the 2022 Oscars. Smith didn't attend the Oscars planning to accost the host (at least by all accounts he didn't). He simply lost it.

Rock made a joke about the actor's wife, Jada Pinkett Smith. Smith wasn't the only actor he made jokes about. He's the emcee of the Academy Awards. That's what he's paid to do. And everyone in the audience knows this is a long-standing part of the show. It's not like Rock suddenly, out of context, singled out Smith, and only Smith, for the one joke of the night. It wasn't personal.

When Rock delivered the punch line, Will Smith appeared to laugh at the joke, but internally, Smith's frustration rapidly boiled over to anger—perhaps egged on by his wife.

Have you ever been offended by something someone said about you or your family? Have you ever felt the heat of rapidly expanding anger upon feeling insulted or disrespected? Have you ever begun to imagine pummeling the crap out of the person who uttered the offensive comment?

If so, you are just like Will Smith, Jeff the airplane guy, and millions of others. It's called being human.

Smith approached the stage, walked up to Rock, and unleashed a furious slap, connecting with Rock's cheek and swiveling his head with its force.

Rock was the opposite of Smith—he neither retaliated nor talked smack about Smith, even weeks afterward. And he didn't retaliate with his own slap.

While the disturbing details of violence we cover in this chapter are shocking—and a departure from the situations we've addressed thus far—the point is that these extremes aren't usually based on some abnormal, malfunctioning mind glitch. Sometimes they are. But many times, they are based on the typical pattern of emotional escalation. And if the violence doesn't happen right away, these feelings of frustration and anger, when not diffused, can continue to build, increasing the risk that the person might erupt in a violent act if triggered.

In this chapter, we'll explore some truly violent acts—a seemingly big leap from the territory we've been exploring in relation to virtual and actual conversations. But, as you'll see, it's not that huge of a leap.

In the Blink of an Eye

On November 13, 2004, Victoria Ruvolo was driving home in Long Island, New York. She had just attended a concert and was only blocks from her house. An oncoming car passed hers; it was a car that would change her life forever.

As that car sped past hers, something happened. It happened so fast she probably didn't know what it was until weeks later, after she emerged from a medically induced coma.

Someone in the passing car had thrown a frozen turkey at Victoria's car. The twenty-pound bird, solid as a rock, was the equivalent of a small boulder striking Victoria's car—and face.

That's right. The frozen turkey struck the windshield, shattered it, and hit the steering wheel with enough force to actually bend and warp the steering wheel, then smash Victoria's face.

There's more to Victoria's story, which I'll tell you in a few minutes. But before I do, I want to talk about love and how hard it sometimes is.

The Heart of the Ruby

I have been thinking about the power of the Platinum and Ruby rules. At their core, I think what I'm really talking about is love.

The heart of the Ruby Rule is loving our fellow human beings who share this planet, even (maybe especially) those who think and feel differently than we do.

I can be civil to and tolerant of others, but love is the only emotion that allows me to be civil to and tolerant of someone spitting in my face—or shattering every bone in my face with a frozen turkey. Love is the only thing that can subvert the natural human response to meet hostility with hostility.

An eye for an eye.

Hit me with a bat, and I'll come back with a knife. Cut me with a knife, and I'll come back with a gun. What you do to me, I'll do back to you—only worse. And that's how this whole vengeance thing escalates.

I occasionally feel that impulse. I think everyone does. But if we are going to learn to get along as humans, we must channel our absolute best and love those who hate us.

I dislike getting preachy, but Jesus and the others, like Buddha, Gandhi, Mandela, Martin Luther King, who taught this concept teach a universal truth: we must learn to love those who hate us and despitefully use us.

It's easy to love your friends but so much harder to love those who hate you.

You know, as I write about forgiving and loving those who hate me, it's easy. It just flows. But it's terrifyingly daunting when I think about implementing it in my life. What about the person on social media who flames my ideas and cusses me out? And then unilaterally reaches out to Instagram and has me canceled? They deserve my contempt and ire. Right? How about the school bully who picks on my son? What about those popular girls who are insanely cruel to my daughter because she doesn't quite fit in? Surely, when someone maliciously hurts your loved one, you are justified in hurting, or at the very least hating, them back. Right?

What about my supposed neighborhood friends who gossip behind my back? Aren't I vindicated in turning a cold shoulder and giving them the evil eye when I see them in their yards? Or ignoring them when they say hi to me as I work in my garage? My behavior is reasonable. Right? I mean, I'm not egging their house or slashing their car tires.

See, when I think of real-world situations I have dealt with, I fall so short. My first reaction is to NOT love them; it's to punch them in the throat, to follow the emperor's advice to Luke as he battles Darth Vader in *Return of the Jedi*: "Use your aggressive feelings, boy. Let the hate flow through you!"[41]

Yeah, I would have totally turned to the dark side, relishing the hate and feeling justified in my pious truth to feed my hatred.

UGH, I've written all these chapters, and now I just feel flat-out hypocritical.

I guess it's true about books and their authors. I need this as much, if not more, than my readers.

So what does it look like when someone not only refuses to hate someone she has every right to despise—but actively loves that person?

Let's go back to our story about Victoria Ruvolo and the frozen turkey.

Kids Being Stupid

Five teenagers were in the car from which the frozen turkey was hurled. College kids. They had just finished being hooligans, using stolen credit cards to buy groceries, games, and movies.[42] One of those groceries was a twenty-pound frozen turkey. According to the driver of the car, Jack Cutrone, he'd bought the turkey to prepare in the dorms since Thanksgiving was a few weeks away.

In the back seat of the car sat eighteen-year-old Ryan Cushing, a college freshman. He thought it would be hilarious to hurl the turkey at the oncoming car. The driver, Cutrone, told police that Cushing hadn't intended to hit the windshield, just the door.

But Cushing did hit the windshield—and the person behind it, Ruvolo. "The impact caused her esophagus to cave in, shattered her cheeks and jaw, and fractured one of her eye sockets. She also suffered brain damage. Ruvolo was in a medically induced coma for two weeks and underwent a 10-hour facial reconstruction surgery along with months of rehabilitation. Doctors at the time said it was a miracle she survived."[43]

Cushing now faced up to twenty-five years in prison for first-degree assault.

In the courtroom, Ruvolo stood and did something extraordinarily difficult for most of us.

She forgave Cushing.

Like, really forgave him.

There will, of course, be some crimes so heinous and some betrayals so devastating and destructive that most of us would be unable to begin the superhuman effort of conjuring any feelings of forgiveness. And I'm just talking about *feeling* forgiveness—not even contacting, encountering, or conveying that sentiment to the perpetrator of such dark acts. And that is perfectly fine. We are, of course, all people who are mostly trying our best to be our best.

Nonetheless, Ruvolo tapped into that elusive inner well that hosts what President Lincoln called "the better angels of our nature."[44]

She persuaded the judge to go easy on Cushing and give him a lighter sentence. The judge was inclined to give this boy the maximum punishment allowed by law, but Ruvolo's riveting and emotional entreaty convinced the judge to agree to a plea bargain for a lesser charge.

"With crime victims, normally they have just the opposite reaction, and death doesn't even satisfy them," Judge Spota said after the hearing. "She [Ruvolo] is just an extraordinary person."[45]

I share this extreme example of forgiveness in contrast with something of which I am guilty, as are perhaps all of us: harboring feelings of animosity toward someone who is not in my political party or who doesn't believe what I believe.

I know I feel this way as I think about all the people who have done me wrong and against whom I still hold grudges. Ruvolo's story is like a string I tie to my finger to remind me not to allow my grudges and resentment toward others—my so-called enemies—to boil over.

In any case, back to the story.

What was the result of Ruvolo's forgiveness? Here's the account of her encounter with her "enemy": "Cushing approached Ruvolo as she left the courtroom and repeatedly told her, 'I'm so sorry,' as he sobbed uncontrollably. Ruvolo reportedly hugged him tight, stroked his face, and patted his back, telling him, 'It's OK, it's OK. I just want you to make your life the best it can be.'"

For Ruvolo, it relieved a potential heavy burden of bitterness, hatred, and desire for revenge. These poison the soul and infect our actions.

For Cushing, he was overwhelmed with genuine sorrow for having hurt Ruvolo and a sincere love for her.

Love spawns more love and positive energy; hate spawns more hate and negative energy.

But it's extraordinarily difficult to let go of our often-justified grievances (and many times unjustified grievances) and forgive someone as an act of love.

Back to Real Life

I'm telling you, it feels really good to hate on dirtbags and unethical people. Forget differences of opinion on politics. I mean, there are people I despise—people who have lied about me, backstabbed me, and sought to ruin my reputation. They deserve my hate, right? Certainly not my love and forgiveness.

Is there someone you hate? Someone who, when you merely think about them, you have a visceral disdain for them? Perhaps somebody who simply aggravates the hell out of you, who you dislike and feel resentment and hostility toward?

I'm guessing we all have one or more of these jokers in our lives.

Now, picture one of the people on your "dirtbag list," then take note of how they instinctively evoke negative, ugly feelings within your soul.

Are you proud of those ugly feelings? Do those feelings make you feel joy, peace, or contentment? Would you encourage your children, significant other, or loved one to follow your example by holding on to and fostering all that hate and anger? Or would you be telling them to let it go? To reach out and make peace?

I have multiple individuals I can think of who cause me to swell with anger, and even hatred and resentment, for things they have done to me. But when I am being candid, I can attest that these feelings are destructive to me and those around me, not to mention being just flat-out counterproductive.

Hate spawns hate and negative energy. It doesn't just corrode you; it seeps out and can be corrosive to those around you.

It's not easy to love your enemy. Trust me, I know. But I ask you—picture the one person you dislike more than any other. See if you can find love for that person. See if you can turn that initial twinge of disgust into something that is not disgust. See if you can move from disgust to something that radiates positivity toward that person.

Now, what if that person tried to stab you to death with a pair of scissors? Could you love your enemy then? Should you?

This next story further examines the question I began to explore in the Victoria Ruvolo story: Are there exceptions to "Love your enemy and forgive those who are downright sinister to you?"

The Limit of Love

Before I jump into this story, I want to reemphasize a point I brought up in the Ruvolo story.

If you are a victim of a heinous crime (e.g., abuse, trafficking, attempted murder, hate crimes, or other vile acts), I'm not advocating for you to hug your enemy and express your love and forgiveness for them as Victoria Ruvolo did to the young man who nearly killed and permanently disfigured her.

I know many people who have undergone such traumas, and they initially misunderstand what I'm talking about in this section. They recoil at the thought of hugging their perpetrators and wishing them well.

I'm not recommending anyone do that. The kid in the Ruvolo story wasn't an abuser, didn't have a criminal background, and wasn't acting with intent to harm a person. He was stupid and impulsive. His act and intentions were very different from those of the malicious, evil criminal whose acts are typically premeditated and serial in nature. If Ruvolo were in court facing a stepfather who had sexually and emotionally abused her for years, I would make an educated guess that she wouldn't give him the warm-fuzzy, hug-and-forgiveness treatment.

In more extreme circumstances, I think learning to love your enemy means examining your hope for them. Do you secretly hope this person rots in hell? Do you covertly or overtly desire that this person feel pain and hurt like you have felt pain and hurt? If so, you have not learned to love your enemy. If you are wishing ill on anyone, even those who hate you, I suggest doing a self-inventory and some meditation. Think about whether it's worth hanging on to and fanning the flames of negative energy. Why? They have the potential to weigh you down and detract from your ability to foster and attract positive energy.

Loving your enemy does not mean putting yourself in a situation where your perpetrators can hurt you again.

For me, it's all about what your heart truly desires for this individual. If you truly hope this person finds deep and lasting change and rehabilitation and can turn their life around and be a kind, loving, trusted, loyal individual, then you are extending love toward that person. But do not blindly ignore the ugly and dangerous characteristics of your enemies and naively treat them as you would a kind neighbor.

With that, let's talk about Yoko's story.

This story takes place in Japan. I am acquainted with some of the people involved, so I won't dive deep into all the details. But I'll give you enough to help you understand my point.

Two high school girls were in a relationship. After five or six months of dating, one of the girls—we'll call her Yoko—discovered her girlfriend was cheating on her.

Yoko's cheating girlfriend ended up trying to kill Yoko, stabbing Yoko twenty-nine times with scissors. The ex-girlfriend thought Yoko was dead, so she waited twenty minutes before calling the police, claiming she had come to visit Yoko (whose parents both worked until late into the evening) only to discover her friend covered in blood and unresponsive in her apartment.

Amazingly, Yoko wasn't dead.

And detectives saw many inconsistencies in the ex-girlfriend's story. And the deal was sealed when Yoko awoke two weeks after surgery and named her ex-girlfriend as her attempted murderer.

Yoko's ex-girlfriend is now in prison, and Yoko still suffers from the physical and mental complications and scars caused by the savage attack.

In a minute, I'll give you some insight into how Yoko felt about her attacker—but first I'd like to explore whether there are times when love and forgiveness are not called for.

Back to the Question:
Is There a Limit to Love and Forgiveness?

Christ and many other religious figures and philosophers have said that we should forgive—even going to the extreme of forgiving and loving our enemies. But can it be done? Are there exceptions to the rule?

In the context of this book, are we able to (and should we) apply the Ruby Rule in all situations? Are there any preexisting conditions that would exempt someone from acting in alignment with any of the rules—Gold, Platinum, or Ruby?

What about in cases of severe abuse, violence, and atrocity? Surely those would be loopholes through which a person could escape the requirement of the Ruby Rule.

And what about people who are so socially nonfunctional they don't even qualify as "human" as we understand it. Psychopaths, sociopaths, narcissists, predators—if your brain is glitched and you don't act within the confines of noncriminal human behavior, do you qualify to have the Ruby Rule applied to you? I mean, if you were to treat a psychopath the way he wants to be treated, wouldn't that mean you would help him find victims and avoid capture? So does the Ruby Rule reach its limit and break down at this point?

To begin to answer this question, I went straight to an expert. I spoke with Yoko about her ordeal and its aftermath. I described the premise of this new book and this chapter in particular. I asked her, "Could you ever truly forgive your ex-girlfriend? Could you love your enemy?"

The paramedics didn't know if Yoko would survive the trip to the hospital. But she did. She spent months in the hospital trying to recover. Some of the deep stabs punctured her intestines, bowels, and bladder, releasing toxins into her body and bloodstream. She went into septic shock, damaging her kidneys and liver. She'll eventually need transplants. As it is now, she suffers from chronic fatigue, frequent nausea, hyper-swollen legs, insomnia, and bouts of severe abdominal pain.

She has also endured several plastic surgeries to reduce the appearance of the slash scars crisscrossing her face. Some of those deep facial cuts and stabs permanently damaged nerves and musculature. It's difficult for her to speak, eat, and drink. She's gone through years of physical and emotional therapy.

During our chat, she told me there was no way she could ever see herself going all-in on loving and forgiving her ex. I explained to her what I explained at the beginning of the previous section, that learning to love your enemy means examining your hope for them. Loving your enemy does not mean putting yourself in a situation where your perpetrator can hurt you again. It's about truly hoping this person finds deep and lasting change and rehabilitation and can turn their life around. That is extending a type of love toward that person.

(In the next chapter, I'll outline ten "Love Your Enemy Hacks"; I previewed them with Yoko, but she said she couldn't accomplish any of them in dealing with her ex, who, thankfully, is behind bars for a very long time).

She just felt it was too much, too far, and too unrealistic. And I get that. And I'm not judging her or anyone else who feels the same way.

She felt that allowing herself to be vulnerable, with an open, soft heart, would encourage her ex's narcissistic tendencies and she would use her kindness against her.

So, I ask myself, is this "love your enemies" thing reserved only for those who kinda sorta hurt you but don't hurt you too bad?

If I think about this to the extreme, what if someone raped and murdered my daughter, mother, or wife? Could I really forgive the rapist?

As I thought of Yoko and her horrific ordeal, I tried to mentally shift into her shoes and walk in them. I wanted to see things from her perspective. I call this being a "shoe-shifter." It's like being a shape-shifter. I define it as having the ability to reshape one's point of view into another's. I'll talk more about shoe-shifting soon.

I tried to feel her pain. I tried to feel the anguish of being betrayed by someone you love—first through infidelity, then through murderous violence.

Yoko claims not to hate her ex-girlfriend. But she definitely doesn't want anything to do with her. Yoko even recoils when someone mentions her ex's name.

I asked her if she was still allowing her ex and memories of her ex to taunt, control, and hold her captive. She said, "In a way, yes. But in another way, my negative gut reaction also protects me and reminds me never to allow her to be in a position where she can perpetrate that kind of evil on me."

Again, this love-your-enemy concept is so, so easy to write about yet so exceptionally difficult to implement. We all have to walk our own path at our own speed. This path of loving your enemies is yours and yours alone. Others can walk beside you, but no one can walk it for you.

I suppose for all those out there who make hideous, subhuman decisions that profoundly damage and harm those around them, we could apply the Ruby and Platinum rules by treating them like the human they *would be* if they weren't defective. If that part of their brain functioned properly, they would want you to desire them to feel remorse, express contrition, and seek and succeed at rehabilitation.

In the case of Yoko, when she testified against her ex-girlfriend, she felt she was actually helping her—putting her in a place where she couldn't harm more innocent people, a place where prison psychologists and therapists could at least try to make some progress in moving the needle on this woman's savage pathologies.

Forgiving doesn't mean you have to give your perpetrator the Ruvolo treatment. Victoria Ruvolo, you'll remember, hugged the teen who crushed her face. She convinced the judge to give the kid a light sentence and told the young man how much she loved him.

You don't have to—nor should you—do that to your abuser, attacker, or predator. All you have to do is relinquish your anger and desire for revenge against them. That is how you can express the type of love Christ and others speak of when they ask humans to love their enemies. *And that serves you as much as or more than the recipient of your forgiveness.* That's why we should seek such an outcome, even in the most extreme cases. Why? Because it's how a victim stabs the specter of their tormentor's influence on them through the heart. It's powerful mojo. And if you can pull it off—though it's perhaps one of the most difficult things in the world to accomplish—it can liberate you.

Chapter Recap

- At the core of the Ruby Rule—the natural, expanding progression of the Golden and Platinum rules—is love. I believe it is about loving our fellow human beings who share this planet, even (maybe especially) those who think and feel differently than we do.

- Usually, the "love your enemy" philosophy and practice applies to situations that involve unkind, uncivil feelings and conversations with others. On occasion, however, it may apply to everyday humans who rapidly escalate from emotional response to violent action.

- Love is the only thing that can subvert the natural human response (an eye for an eye) to hostility toward us.

- Love spawns more love and positive energy; hate spawns more hate and negative energy.

- Hate doesn't just corrode you; it seeps out and can be corrosive to those around you.

- The concept of "love your enemy" is easy to write about yet exceptionally difficult to implement.

- You can't dispel anger with more anger.

Pause and Think

- Is there anybody you hate? Someone who, when you merely think about them, results in visceral disdain? Perhaps somebody who simply aggravates the hell out of you, who you dislike and feel resentment and hostility toward? Could you mentally entertain the thought of loving them?

- Do those feelings bring joy, peace, or contentment? Would you encourage your children, significant other, or loved one to follow your example by holding on to and fostering all those negative feelings? Or would you be telling them to let it go? To reach out and make peace?

- Are there exceptions to the rule, "Love your enemy and forgive those who do you wrong"?

CHAPTER 6

TEN "LOVE YOUR ENEMY" HACKS
Because We Need All the Help We Can Get

L et's assume loving your enemy is a worthy goal. So how do you follow this teaching? I am looking for tangible ways I can start to change my heart concerning my enemies. And I mean I. I need to start with these. Like I said early in this book, I need this read as much, if not more, than others.

But first, a quick disclaimer before jumping into the heart of this chapter. These hacks for loving your enemy are geared toward "enemies" who have become enemies based on, typically, much simpler issues (like a neighbor treating you unfairly or someone with a starkly different political opinion or a person with an offensive post on social media) than we covered in the previous chapter.

In the previous chapter, we looked at some heavy, serious, disturbing issues. If you happen to be dealing with current or past instances of some of these issues (e.g., child abuse, sexual assault, narcissism, domestic violence, and others), I strongly encourage you to seek professionally trained and experienced counselors, if you haven't already. I believe the ideas in this chapter and in the entire book can help you; however, in such situations, I consider these ideas supplementary to the profes-sional counseling you may receive.

And if you find yourself chronically angry, even without seeming cause, you might consider seeking professional help.

Love Is the Only Way Forward

Do you find yourself feeling angry toward others?

Maybe your stepfather is mean, your buddy flirts with your girlfriend, your coworker stabs you in the back, or your neighbor is a hard-core Democrat and you are a staunch Republican—and you've had some heated debates and cold shoulders.

Time passes, and you say, "It's cool. I'm good. I got this." Then one day, WHAM! There they are in front of you in the checkout line and you can't control it. You want to punch their smug face.

They did something hurtful and mean, and now you're angry with them. What they did was wrong.

But did you know that even when you're justified in having negative feelings toward an individual, if you hold on to those negative feelings, it ends up hurting you, not them? It's unhealthy, and you won't find deep happiness until you release those negative vibes.

Easier said than done.

Others will hurt you; whether intentionally or unintentionally, the pain is the same. With that in mind, here are four big ideas on love and hate. I guess you could call these the rationale behind practicing the love-your-enemy hacks.

1. When you hate others, you hate yourself by allowing the darkness to live inside you. LOVE YOU more than you HATE OTHERS.

2. To love, you must forgive. If you don't, you live imprisoned in the past, unable to enjoy the present.

3. Hatred is an individual dilemma that swells into a global crisis. Look around; ignorance, arrogance, and hate are everywhere.

4. Loving someone who does not love you back is a test of YOUR character, not theirs.

With that being said, here are a few loving-my-enemy hacks I'm working on. Notice I said I'm *working* on these hacks. I haven't mastered them—nor have I tried, failed, and simply given up. It's a work in progress, probably a lifelong pursuit, never truly perfected but constantly practiced and refined. I had to specify that I'm still working on this because I can envision my wife glaring at me as she reads this. She, better than anyone, knows how imperfect I am and how much I need to learn to walk my talk. Again, I am—we all are—a work in progress.

If any or all these hacks resonate with you, please give them a test drive. Together, we can make a small dent in a world inexplicably bent on dividing us.

1. Pause, Breathe, and Count to Ten

This is an oldie but goodie. And now it's backed by science showing that breathing exercises can reduce stress and induce emotional calm.

When he wasn't writing constitutions and founding universities, Thomas Jefferson was apparently breathing and counting to ten. "When angry," he said, "count to 10 before you speak; if very angry, a hundred."[46]

This hack helps you get centered by forcing you to hit the pause button on reacting and slow down.

If you find yourself thinking about your "enemy," you likely feel anger, contempt, and even hatred. Work toward not allowing those feelings to control you and dictate your actions. This exercise can be a simple first step toward that goal.

Pay attention to your feelings. When thoughts of your enemy swarm your brain and your feelings drift into negative territory,

take a deep breath, count to ten, then emotionally and/or physically step back from the precipice of plunging into the murky
muck of negativity.

Try to let go of your body. Imagine yourself floating in the
air as an objective spectator, an observer. You are no longer you;
instead, you're simply watching.

This mental game can help you see the situation dispassion-
ately. Because we all know that when we're caught up in the
intensity and swing of our emotions, it's virtually impossible to
be objective.

Why does counting to ten work?

Counting to ten not only delays you from lashing out or
letting your anger intensify, it provides a distraction from the
anger-arousing incident. While you are busy counting, you're
not stoking the flames of anger until they rage out of control.

Take slow, deep breaths between each number. Deep breathing helps counter the fight-or-flight stress response that underlies anger. Deep, slow breathing can bring a sense of relaxation
and help you focus on the present moment.

Not only that, but slow, deep breathing can also bring
about meaningful health benefits as well as emotional benefits.
Researchers don't know exactly why this happens, but this is one
of many interesting hypotheses:

> One promising idea focuses on the sensory nerves around
> the chest—the effects of which we feel whenever we fill
> our lungs to the max. "You can tell just by taking a deep
> breath how much it is a mechanical act," explains Don-
> ald Noble at Emory University in the U.S. That feeling of
> pressure comes from a set of stretchy sensors that gauge
> the expansion of the lungs. The chest movement pro-
> duced by the relaxation of the diaphragm when we exhale

also places pressure on the blood vessels feeding into the heart, ultimately triggering another set of sensors (called baroreceptors) in our arteries.

Both types of sensors feed into the brainstem, and Noble proposes that when we take deep breaths, the activity in other regions might synchronize with that steady, repetitive stimulation. The resulting slow brain waves lead us into a state of relaxed alertness. Quicker, shallower breaths simply don't stimulate those nerves— or the brain—so effectively; you need a long inhalation and exhalation to generate the right brain rhythms.

Just as importantly, the pressure-sensitive baroreceptors, in the arteries around the heart, feed into the vagus nerve. This is an essential element of the nervous system that is thought to be particularly important in dampening the fight-or-flight response after a threat has disappeared. "It allows the body to focus on things that are basically restorative or nourishing," says Noble—a state that is often known as "rest-and-digest." By repeatedly stimulating the vagus nerve during those long exhalations, slow breathing may shift the nervous system towards that more restful state, resulting in positive changes like a lower heart rate and lower blood pressure.[47]

A great way to measure your deep breathing (and give you something to focus on other than your anger or negative energy) is the 4-7-8 method. It's pretty simple. You inhale for 4 seconds, hold your breath for 7 seconds, and exhale for 8 seconds. That can count as one rep of your 10 as you count to 10.

According to *Medical News Today,* "Dr. Andrew Weil teaches the 4-7-8 breathing technique, which he believes can help with the following: reducing anxiety, helping a person get to sleep, managing cravings, or reducing anger responses."[48]

The article goes on to say:

A person may feel lightheaded after doing this for the first few times. Therefore, it is advisable to try this technique when sitting or lying down to prevent dizziness or falls.

The total number of seconds that the pattern lasts for is less important than keeping the ratio. A person who cannot hold their breath for long enough may try a shorter pattern instead, such as:

breathe in through the nose for 2 seconds
hold the breath for a count of 3.5 seconds
exhale through the mouth for 4 seconds.[49]

As with most things nowadays, there are apps to help you time your breathing.

Anger is impulsive. That's why most people can control their impulses if they can buy themselves time through distraction. Unfortunately, we can't eliminate anger from our lives. The key is to check our anger as it sprouts and before it can grow and mature.

2. Shoe-Shifting—Put Yourself in Their Shoes

To paraphrase F. Scott Fitzgerald, the test of human intelligence is being able to retain two opposing ideas at once and still function.[50]

In other words, empathy can be measured by the ability to simultaneously think from two opposing perspectives and retain your ability to calmly and rationally think for yourself.

It simply describes trying to walk in someone else's shoes.

The ability to walk in another's shoes is an extraordinary skill. It's almost as magical as the shape-shifters in those sci-fi fantasies. In this case, I am coining a term to describe the act of trying to walk in someone else's shoes for a while and empathetically see things from their point of view. I call it becoming a shoe-shifter.

If you think being a shoe-shifter is hard on its own, try shoe-shifting into an enemy's point of view.

It's crazy-hard to do, but this hack might be able to help you get there.

In a proper shoe-shift, you try to remove yourself from a given situation (in-person interactions, interactions through media, or interactions that take place in our minds) and look at that situation from above. If it sounds like I'm describing an out-of-body experience, bingo. That's the goal of being a shoe-shifter.

Pretend you're levitating above the situation. Then try to look down into the body and head of your enemy.

It sounds kind of creepy when I say it like that, but I'm not talking about X-ray vision, astral projection, or soul-hopping.

What I'm talking about is imagining yourself as that person. What makes that person who they are? What types of events might have shaped their beliefs? What are they going through right now? What made them do what they did? How did they feel about it all?

You will need to use your imagination and see this person as a human being. You'll need to humanize them. Dehumanizing a person makes it much easier to hate them. If you can make someone seem less than human or hardly human at all, it's easier to justify hatred and even violence toward them. That's why despots and dictators make dehumanizing others the first goal of their propaganda and how psychopaths, sociopaths, and narcissists can hurt others so badly. They see others as objects.

Once you're able to humanize your enemy, you can view them through the lens of what you know about humans. Human beings strive to do good but make mistakes and have different perspectives. And because they have different perspectives, it's essential to see the situation from the perspective of another person to humanize them further.

If you are successful in your shoe-shift, you will learn that no one has it easy. Everyone is fighting a battle you know nothing about. You just never know what others are going through . . . just like I was unaware of the situation of the driver I encountered on I-15 so long ago. He wasn't a reckless driver priding himself on being able to pass everyone else in the traffic jam; he was a father speeding along the shoulder so he could get to the hospital in time to see his wife.

So, to review, pause and count to ten before you start judging, criticizing, or letting the anger build. Then, in that calmer state of mind, try shoe-shifting into your enemy's point of view. It's the only way to start turning contempt into empathy and empathy into love.

3. Seek to Understand

Empathetic understanding is the goal of becoming a shoe-shifter. I must stress this here because it can go a long way toward helping you understand a person's actions and the reasons behind those actions, even if it's not your desire to really try to understand the person himself.

This hack is based on a concept that should be familiar to those of you who are Stephen Covey fans. He said, "If I were to summarize in one sentence the single most important principle I have learned in the field of interpersonal relations, it would be this: Seek first to understand, then to be understood."[51] (This is Covey's habit number five, if you were wondering.)

Most seek first to be understood—and care little, if at all, about what others believe. This is because, clearly, they know the truth based on instant certainty, which is never wrong. These people want to make sure everyone sees it the way they see it.

And in doing so, they ignore what others are seeing or saying.

Oh, they smile, look others in the eye, nod their heads, and throw in a few uh-huhs now and then. Still, most only pretend to listen. They selectively hear certain parts of the conversation but miss the overall meaning.

Why is this the norm?

Because most everyone is listening with the purpose to respond, not to understand. They listen as they mentally prepare what they're going to say. They filter everything they hear through their perspective. They check what they hear against the world they know. Accordingly, they decide impulsively what the other person means and believes before their counterpart has finished speaking.

Some of you might be thinking, *What if I make an effort to listen and understand, but the person I'm engaging with does not?*

Great question. In my humble opinion, one person who is genuinely listening is better than none.

My experience is that if I genuinely shoe-shift and use empathetic listening, it usually leads those with opposing viewpoints to soften their approach and listen more intently to my thoughts. If I listen to you, you are more likely to do the same for me. We can be the examples whose actions help others learn and see the power in this approach.

In other words, by truly listening to and hearing you, I'm treating you as you would like to be treated. This is the Platinum Rule at its best, and from there you can lean into the Ruby Rule. I believe this is the antidote to the poison of rage and hate polluting our politics and national dialogue, from the smallest and most personal level to the broadest, nationwide level.

Real understanding is a sign that you are listening to what the other person has to say. It's what we all desire—to be understood and valued and affirmed. Seeking to understand others is a critical step in jarring you out of your "enemy" state of mind and allowing you to move toward turning an enemy into a friend.

4. Accept Them As They Are

Acceptance of others is a difficult but critical step because you can't love someone you refuse to accept.

Accept an enemy as they are instead of trying to change them. Accept the fact that this person is who they are.

Let me frame this another way. Have you ever tried to change someone you love?

Maybe your child is lazy or on social media too much, or your significant other is messy and disorganized. Perhaps they'd rather stay in at night and chill rather than go out on the town, or they are interested in topics and activities that make no sense to you. Whatever it is, you'd like to change them.

Does it work? Or did it work when you tried it?

Let me be very clear: Stop. Doing. That.

It seldom works, and it causes harmful amounts of stress, anger, resentment, and frustration—for both parties.

My point is this: If you can't change someone you care about, do you think you can ever change your enemy?

There have been times when I was guilty of trying to change those around me. I confess that I never admitted I was trying to change them. No way! Not me. I'm not that kind of guy. I'm a motivator, after all. I was merely trying to "encourage," "persuade," and "inspire" them to be the best person they could be.

But let's be honest here: I was trying to change them. I was fooling myself and trying to deceive them into thinking otherwise.

Your energy and time are better spent on changing you.

Improve yourself—mind, spirit, body, and actions.

Remember the Platinum Rule: Treat others the way *they* would like to be treated. Do you really believe others around you want you to step in and try to change them? Come on, really? And forget about making the leap to the Ruby Rule if you are still struggling with the Platinum Rule.

Trying to change someone else is like trying to hold a beach ball under the water. It is possible with a great deal of force and effort, temporarily, but that beach ball will eventually pop back up to the surface. So you effectively waste your time if you think you can keep that ball submerged—or try to make someone change.

Focus on you. Manage you.

I have never met anyone who wants to be managed (which is like trying to change someone), and, likewise, I have never met anyone who doesn't want to be led (which is focusing on *you* to the point where others want to follow you).

Be your best self. Encourage others. Inspire them. Be a role model. Others will admire you, and hopefully they will want to emulate you. Don't be discouraged if others don't want to change. Just accept them as they are and let them marvel as you change. Shrug it off and keep being the awesome person you are. That's all you can do.

5. Forgive and Forget the Past

Forgive?

This is one difficult step. But I'm sure you already know this. Unless you're very different from most other people, you've had experience with being hurt, physically or emotionally, and have had to struggle with the concept of forgiveness. When that happens, *forgiveness* moves from a concept to something real.

Is it possible to truly forgive your enemy for what they've done?

It should be relatively easier to forgive someone if you have successfully practiced the mental trick of detaching yourself from the situation—because what has happened is now in the past.

No matter how much it hurts or you don't like it, it can't be changed. So you have come to a fork in the road and must make a choice: either you hate what has happened in the past and let the anger eat at your soul, or you accept it and work on those things you can control—yourself and your future.

It's okay to let it go. Give yourself permission to do it. It will only eat at you if you don't. Let go of the past and let go of your feelings of contempt for this person. These negative feelings can do nothing but hurt you.

You *do* have the ability to forgive. But to be happy and at peace with yourself, you must let go of past hurts.

Letting go is not easy. In fact, it's dauntingly, painfully difficult. Because you feel justified in your anger. And you probably are justified.

But forgiving is essential for long-term emotional and mental health.

REMEMBER! Forgiving doesn't mean denying someone's responsibility for your hurt, nor does it mean you minimize or justify the act. That's NOT what I'm talking about at all.

What I'm talking about is the act of allowing yourself to forgive, to let go and move on without condoning or excusing what they did.

Forgiveness is a choice. And it's entirely up to you. We all have the right to feel resentment. But on the flip side of that, we all have the right to choose NOT to feel resentment.

When you forgive, you refuse to be the victim, and you let go of any control or power the offending person/situation has over you. You refuse to allow hurt, grudges, or other wrongdoings to dictate your life and how you live.

The act of forgiving is the ultimate release from past pain, memories, and enslavement.

If you refuse to forgive, you allow the past to consume you to the point that you give up control. As a result, you can carry anger, bitterness, and resentment into the future, and that can cause problems in your relationships. This can also lead to robbing you of the peace of mind, health, and happiness you desire.

The benefits you gain from forgiving and letting go are numerous. Here are a few:

- Positive thoughts, feelings, and actions begin to reemerge and flourish, promoting psychological well-being.

- Stress, anxiety, depression, and chronic pain can be eased.

- You experience greater compassion, understanding, and healing.

- You have less illness (thanks to reduced stress).

- You have a lower risk of substance abuse and alcoholism.

- You have the ability to perform better at your job and/or in your education.

- You'll feel an increased sense of optimism and hope for the future.

We could go on, but I think you get the picture. Forgiving is good for you mentally, emotionally, and physically.

Dr. Martin Luther King said in a sermon he titled, "Loving Your Enemies":

There's another reason why you should love your enemies, and that is because hate distorts the personality of the hater.

We usually think of what hate does for the individual hated or the individuals hated or the groups hated. But it is even more tragic; it is even more ruinous and injurious to the individual who hates. You just begin hating somebody, and you will begin to do irrational things. You can't see straight when you hate. You can't walk straight when you hate. You can't stand upright. Your vision is distorted. There is nothing more tragic than to see an individual whose heart is filled with hate. He comes to the point that he becomes a pathological case. For the person who hates, you can stand up and see a person, and that person can be beautiful, and you will call them ugly. For the person who hates, the beautiful becomes ugly, and the ugly becomes beautiful. For the person who hates, the good becomes bad, and the bad becomes good. For the person who hates, the true becomes false, and the false becomes true. That's what hate does. You can't see right. The symbol of objectivity is lost. Hate destroys the very structure of the personality of the hater.[52]

6. Look for the Good in Them

You've succeeded in forgiving someone and relinquishing hate, but that's only part of the process. Simply giving up hate, while good for you and the world around you, is not enough. It leaves you with feelings of neutrality. Sure, there is no more hate, but there is most likely nothing in its place. If you are doing this right, you replace hate with love. You are not satisfied with a void of nothingness.

So how can you replace hate with love?

Start by finding something you admire in that person.

It could be anything: their smile, their willingness to help others, their love for their family, or their tenacity in standing up for what they believe in, even if it is opposite of what you believe.

If you humbly look hard enough, you will find something decent in everyone—even those you believe are completely void of any redeeming value. You might have to take your time as a shoe-shifter and really get to know the person, which can be difficult. It was Abraham Lincoln who said, "I don't like that man. I must get to know him better."[53]

One little trick I like to use for this is what I call "scaling." How awful a human being is your enemy? Rate them on a scale of one to ten, with one being not too awful and ten being satanically AWFUL.

Perhaps you don't like the person you're thinking of because they gave you a dirty look at the store or ignored you at a party. That might be a one. At the other end of the scale, a ten would be the vilest, most despicable person you can think of. A rating of ten is for the Hitlers, Stalins, Pol Pots, and Mehmet Talaat Pashas of the world.

How evil is your enemy, really? If your enemy is a five, why do you have emotional reactions that are a nine (or ten!) on the scale of getting insanely upset? It's proportionally imbalanced and not worth the expenditure of energy.

Everyone is not all good, but there is always something good in everyone. We are all sinners; not one of us is perfect. We all have a bit of our past we are not proud of. But the opposite is also true. We can all be saints at times. We all have the ability to forgive, let go, and move on. We all have a future.

Mother Teresa said, "Everybody has something good inside them. Some hide it, some neglect it, but it is there."[54]

7. See Yourself in Them

If number six seems too intangible—you can't think of any redeeming quality in your enemy—it is most likely because you don't know your enemy well enough. Go back and practice being a better shoe-shifter.

Walk their walk. Understand the path they have taken to get where they are. Project yourself into them. Pull out your microscope and train it on the details of their lives—and try to spot any similarities you might share. At first, it may seem you have no similarities at all, but focus that microscope and don't give up.

If you're struggling with this, try finding similarities between them and someone you deeply admire.

As you identify these similarities, you're trying to find something about this enemy that you can love.

You have to reach a point where you can truly identify with this person. You have to see yourself as they see themselves. This is the only way to invoke genuine empathy and love.

8. Seek Common Ground

If you've found some similarities, it's time to begin hiking toward common ground. If you are willing to look for it, there's always something you have in common with someone. That might include shared interests, common experiences growing up, working, or with the people you love. You will be able to relate to them better if you share common ground.

To build friendship and connectivity with people with whom you disagree, try to find common ground when conversing with them.

Make a list. Start a common-ground journal. Observe them for several days or weeks until you're able to come up with at least a few things.

Trust is built when you can connect with someone with whom you have something in common. As an example, food, drinks, exercise, fishing, golfing, and cooking are all activities that create a sense of community, allowing you to converse with others and build trust and human connection.

And trust can lead to friendship, which opens the door to more complex topics you can explore.

Empathy allows you to better understand how others see things. You see that not all their opinions are incorrect and not all yours are correct. You learn to be open-minded. You come to appreciate each other and learn to be open to compromise. You have more tools that allow you to solve previous problems.

9. Have an Open, Soft Heart

Like all the hacks that came before, this one is difficult for me. I'm thinking of a person right now who hurt me. What they did was wrong. And I feel my heart constrict as I write this and think of them.

You see, even after accomplishing hacks one through eight, you can experience a relapse. Something can trigger a return of negative feelings toward your enemy and knock you back to square one. If you don't train your heart to be open and accepting and tender, you might give up on this quixotic quest and just say, "Bag it! I really like hating on my enemies! I'm reverting to the comfy state that lets me reach out and do something uncomfortably scary."

I close and harden my heart to those I don't like as a method of emotional self-preservation. I can make believe I have an open heart toward them, but there is a bit of hypocrisy in this pretense. My heart is trying to protect me. I (like most everyone I know) fear vulnerability, rejection, and being hurt. My closed-off heart can be remarkably effective in protecting me against these things—but it also prevents my happiness at times. It prevents me from forming relationships. It prevents me from loving and finding love.

Again, go back to the lesson taught by Christ about loving your enemy. It is easy to open your heart to your neighbor, but what about your enemy?

If you only open your heart to family and friends, you limit your joy. You limit yourself. Your enemy is not limiting you; *you* are limiting you.

As I said, I still need a lot of practice with this philosophy. But I will try to open my heart to a former enemy, even if it is a tiny step at a time. I must; I know it is the only way I will find love for that self-righteous pompous jerk (Oops, did I just say that? See how hard this is? UGH!).

I'd encourage you to do the same, starting with a tiny step.

10. Reach Out to Them

It is one thing to love someone but quite another to show that love in a meaningful way. There are many ways to show someone your love: telling them, smiling at them, laughing with them, sharing your thoughts with them, and having open conversations about how you feel.

When it comes to love and virtue, think unilaterally. Walk your path and live your code of ethics—even when others don't. This will create positive feelings in you, even if others sink in their own quicksand of negativity.

Others will respect you. You'll create the best chance that your enemy will treat you better in the future.

All you can do is what you can do. Be at peace. Others will do whatever they are going to do, and I promise it will not always be that great or pleasant. We all fall short. We all have a million thoughts spinning in our heads; life, at times, is hard, our ethics get fuzzy, our thinking gets clouded. Welcome to the real world. (Spoiler alert: It will never be perfect!)

You will never find peace out in the world; you have to find peace in your heart. And you will experience peace in your heart only when you keep your eyes and heart open, doing good whenever and however you can and continuing to let go along the way.

I recently practiced this principle, though not because I'm totally awesome at letting go of hard feelings. Instead, it's because I'm writing about reaching out to others with whom you have a beef, and suddenly I felt kinda hypocritical for advising others to do this stuff while I was still stewing over getting screwed by certain folks.

I committed to letting go, so I could take that leap of faith, reach out, and tell them I held no ill will toward them—despite my anger and contempt, which was justified by their harmful, hurtful, unethical, and/or potentially illegal actions toward me.

This was hard for me, just like it might be hard for you. I really did hold some bitter feelings in my heart toward them. Letting go of those feelings frightened me. It felt so good to stoke the flames of my anger against them. It felt good to resent them. Intellectually, I knew I was only hurting and limiting myself with the anger I carried in my heart, but emotionally, I knew I really, really, really loved hatin' on these dirtbags.

Nonetheless, I decided to try this stuff out. Really try it. It wasn't that I wanted to show off or set myself up as the end-all, be-all example of this. In fact, quite the opposite. I decided to do this because I felt a bit hollow writing about my theories and philosophies without having put this principle into practice.

So, with that in mind and knowing I dreaded making the plunge into loving my enemies instead of harboring hate and resentment, here's what I wrote to one of them:

I am reaching out as a neighbor in the community and an acquaintance that sees you around town from time to time. I want you to know I hold no ill will toward you. Although, I will confess this has not always been the case. That is my bad.

Next time I see you (or you see me) in a grocery store, or anywhere else, please feel free to say hello. I will do the same.

Gulp.

I'd really rather just write about this stuff and not have to live it.

Or would I?

My nemesis instantly wrote back that he was grateful I had written him and he held no ill will toward me. He hoped things would be different between us, and he appreciated my efforts to make that happen.

To which I replied, "I appreciate the reply. I see no reason we cannot be friends."

A few days after I wrote that last note, something remarkable happened.

The garage door was open as I worked in my woodshop one morning, and I saw this individual, the very person I'd held such contempt for all these years—you know, the one I emailed and tried to forgive.

Remember, I'd spent years cultivating my negative feelings and visceral anger for this person. And I'd felt justified in doing so. Really justified. I'd clung to the resentment and stored it in my soul and weirdly felt good about it. Why? I felt I had every right to level my anger at him. How would one email (one very hard-to-write email that made me cringe with every keystroke) change any of that? I mean, how could one email substantively change me?

I had not seen this guy in years, but that morning in the woodshop, I looked through the open door, and there he was.

Before our short email exchange, seeing him would have caused my heart to instantly flood with anger. I would have seethed and been ready for a verbal altercation. At the very least, I would have fantasized about what demeaning things I could say to him to cut him down to size. I would have glared at him and dared him to approach.

I mean, I know all this because I've thought of him or seen him from time to time over the years, and that's exactly how I reacted. It was a predictable, Pavlovian response.

But, to my amazement, when I looked up and saw him through my open garage door, none of that happened. Because of the email exchange, I felt no anger—none of that escalating negativity that feeds off itself until it's like a volcano ready to erupt.

He never came over and said hello. But I was amazed at the lack of negative energy I felt toward him.

It felt peculiar, to be honest, so bizarre I had to go in and share the experience with my wife.

It was a surreal and strangely freeing sensation I can't quite describe. My anger was no longer there.

I think about how I carried these negative feelings toward this guy for years. Now there is a peace that feels like I had been walking around with a massive sliver in my foot—and rather than removing the sliver, I was content to live with the pain and discomfort it caused. But now the sliver is out. There is still pain because the wound hasn't had a chance to heal, but the point is, the wound now has a *chance* to heal, where it didn't before.

The reality is that you can't dispel anger with anger. You can't put out a fire with more fuel. You have to put out the fire of anger by not feeding it. For years I fed the fire with a fuel of my own making, a fire that blazed within me for years, and it hurt no one but me.

It's sad when I think of it now. What could I have done with that energy had I dropped the anger long ago? Instead of feeding my anger, I could have been feeding my soul with loving, positive thoughts that created loving, positive actions.

While I can reflect on it, I can't change the past. But I *can* be grateful that at least I'm not carrying that anger any longer.

Instead of adding another angry voice to a conflict, aim to be the balm of sweetness that cools others' tempers. Anger drains you. Holding contempt in your heart exhausts your energy and depletes your resources. Trust me, I know that firsthand. If you respond to situations lovingly, you will be filled with harmony, positive energy, and peace. I can attest to that with my own simple example.

I suspect that for most people reading this, this seems like a do-able goal. It's not an easy goal, as I can confirm from my encounter through that open garage door. But it *is* a do-able goal.

Once I let go of my anger toward my neighbor, I felt released from bondage to my animalistic rage and hatred. I felt lighter. I felt like this guy—this former nemesis—no longer controlled my reactions or how I felt. I cut the ties of the emotional puppet master. I'm sure he had no clue I was giving him this control. I am sure he was not oblivious to my contempt for him. I hypothesize that reaching out to others works when it comes to forgiving the slightest transgressions as well as the biggest offenses.

The Ripple Effect

Anger and kindness are both like rocks you can throw into a lake. Both have the power to create a ripple effect that spreads to others. As I wrote this chapter and reflected on the anger I felt, I thought about the negative ripples I generated for years with that anger.

And I thought about the positive ripples a profound act of love and forgiveness can produce.

To better illustrate my point, I offer exhibit A, or ripple 1: my wife.

After I shared my experience in the woodshop with my wife, she told me she needed to follow my example.

That was a hoot.

She is the most loving, forgiving, kindest person on the planet. I'm not exaggerating. So when she said this, I was a bit taken aback. But she told me that watching me go through this and eating my own dog food, so to speak, touched her, and she needed to take similar action toward those for whom she carried negative feelings.

That simple act caused one small ripple. Who knows how far it will travel throughout the world? Regardless of how many people it touches, I'm grateful I was able to be part of it.

And I think that's what this whole thing is about. We have so much animosity festering in the country—in our neighborhoods, on the airwaves, and on social media—that the only way to turn the tide against it, and perhaps literally save our republic, is at the individual level. So we must live the best parts of the Golden and Platinum rules and hopefully begin to practice the Ruby Rule in all we do. As part of that, we must love our enemies.

It's incredibly difficult, but the fruits it bears are worth it.

Chapter Recap

- Pause, breathe, and count to ten.
- Put yourself in someone else's shoes (shoe-shifting).
- Seek to understand.
- Accept others as they are.

- Forgive others and forget the past.

- Look for the good in others.

- See yourself in others.

- Seek common ground.

- Have an open, soft heart.

- Reach out to others.

- Remember that anger and kindness are both like rocks you can throw into a lake; both have the power to create a ripple effect that spreads to others.

Pause and Think

- Is there someone who bugs you to the core and makes your skin crawl just hearing their name? How much negative energy are you holding on to because you refuse to let go?

- Set a goal to begin putting these principles to the test. Choose an enemy and choose a hack from the list. Try the hack. Work on it. Journal your experience and track your thoughts about the experiment and about your enemy over the next two to four weeks. Go back and reread these entries after two to four weeks. Do you notice any evolution in your insights and thoughts?

- Regardless of whether you feel you've accomplished the one hack you tried, choose another and give it a shot. Repeat your journaling pattern.

- Here's another shoe-shifting experiment. Consider: What if you're the one someone else is trying to love? What if you're the enemy? Can you recognize that and be humble enough to allow others to implement these hacks on you?

- As an experiment, choose one person who causes you to feel disdain, aggravation, or serious anger. Consider reaching out and telling them you have no hard feelings toward them. See if this act of love turns out to be a bigger gift to you than to them. Does the act sever their control over how angry they make you feel?

- Journal about your experiment. What would you do differently? Would you do it again? How did it make you feel—before, during, and after—to reach out to one of the people who really bother you?

CHAPTER 7

LIGHT VERSUS DARK

Scatter the Darkness with Light

Everything I needed to know about the forces of light and dark I learned from *Star Wars*.

The idea is simple. There are two main forces at play in the universe: the light side and the dark side. Put another way, there is positive energy and negative energy.

Positive energy is born of and generates goodness, kindness, love, and charity. The negative energy symbolized by Darth Vader's dark side is born of and generates evil, hatred, anger, and revenge. Both sides fuel the human psyche and spawn corresponding actions. But ultimately, one is more powerful than the other and prevails amid all the conflicts between light and dark: the forces of light and positive energy. Sometimes it prevails right away; sometimes it takes awhile.

Of course, we all know it's not as simple as that. The binary of right or wrong, good or bad, is not adequate to describe the subtleties and intricacies of human relations.

We often see the world as right and left, hate and love, good and bad. This is what allows the extreme fringes to believe they are right and everyone else is wrong—and to scream the loudest about it.

But the reality is that our world is not always easily distilled into unambiguous states of right or wrong. Sometimes it can be. But many times, we get ambiguity and varying shades of gray.

If you watch the major news channels (on both sides), you'll quickly see that they use the false binary of right and wrong or good and evil to manipulate the ideas and actions of their viewers.

Their subtext: If you are on the side of light—if you're good—you think like us. Those who don't think like us are minions of the dark side.

As we start this discussion, I'll be using the metaphor of night and day and light and dark as artists and authors do to make a point about civility. Remember, though; I'm not declaring a good-bad binary. I acknowledge that there are unending shades of gray.

Good starting point? Then let's begin our examination of what this has to do with civility and your participation in acts of civility.

"These Stupid Drivers Are Getting on My Nerves. Idiots."

A few nights ago, I was driving home with my wife. The last vestiges of sunset had faded, and moonlight had taken the sky.

We were on a rural, two-lane road that cut through the countryside, winding side to side and rolling over hills. I was in pretty good spirits at first, but I was rapidly getting irked.

Other drivers kept nailing me in the retinas with their high beams.

Which, of course, temporarily blinded me each time.

If it had happened once, I probably would have brushed it off. If it had happened twice, I probably would have been slightly annoyed. But it seemed like every time we crested a hill, someone flashed me with their high beams. I was getting more and more irritated. I expressed this growing hostility to my wife in my gruff, growly way. "These stupid drivers are getting on my nerves. Idiots!"

My wife softly asked, "Art, do you have your lights on?"

I rolled my eyes. What a dumb question! Of course, I had my lights on. I wished she would just join me in hating on these other drivers instead of trying to point the finger at me, when clearly—

At that moment, I glanced down at the dashboard.

I hadn't turned on my headlights.

As it turns out, all those other drivers who had been flashing their high beams at me hadn't been stupid idiots. They weren't ignorant, hostile, or inconsiderate. Nope, they were trying to help me. They had *my* best interests in mind. They wanted me to emerge from the dangerous darkness I was driving in by illuminating my own light to scatter the darkness before me. That, by the way, was very Ruby Rule of them.

I felt small and sheepish. Turns out, I was the idiot here.

(By the way, this was another prime example of instant certainty on my part. When my wife suggested a possibility I simply KNEW couldn't be the truth, I dismissed it for a moment or two without even bothering to consider that she—and all those other drivers—may be right and I may be wrong.)

When I realized I had been barreling down the dark road at high speeds without headlights, I got the heebie-jeebies. What I'd been doing was totally dangerous. I'm lucky I didn't crash or that another car, failing to see me, hadn't sideswiped me or hit me head-on.

Have you ever done that before? Maybe you've had that same experience.

When I turned on my lights, the road was illuminated before

me, and it gave me much peace and comfort. Not only could I see the road, but other cars could now easily see me.

Just as I had no idea I was driving in the darkness without my lights on, I believe many in our society are living in the darkness and instant certainty of hate, anger, hostility, and incivility—and don't even know it.

And just as car after car tried to clue me into the fact that I was in danger but I ignored them, so it is with friends, family, and acquaintances. They may say and do uncivil things that perpetuate negative feelings, distrust, and anger in others around them. Others may try to flash their high beams at them to help them emerge from the darkness, but those engulfed in the darkness of negative energy will most likely get annoyed and brush aside those trying to help.

If we are patient and gently nudge, encourage, and love others, hopefully they will one day look at their dashboards and discover that their lights aren't on. Hopefully, they will discover that it was they who were driving in darkness this whole time.

But you can't force the issue. While trying to inspire others with positive energy, the only thing you can control is strengthening yourself and overcoming your own negativity. The magic will come by your mere example. You can't control others, but you can inspire them.

Physics

In issues of human motivation and action, no one is either all good or all evil. That binary does not exist.

But in physics, light and dark *are* mutually exclusive binaries. Darkness is the total absence of light. The shades of gray between light and dark are simply intensifying or weakening intensities of light.

As metaphors go, light equals positive energy, while darkness equals negative energy. This is virtually universal throughout the history of *Homo sapiens*. Why is that?

Is it a heritage born of our origins, when our evolutionary ancestors knew that more danger arrived with the darkness of night?

Daytime had its dangers, but at least we could see what was coming.

Light, good. Dark, bad . . . even spooky.

Then we invented fire! Or, rather, harnessed fire. And that made the night less spooky, scared away some of the things trying to eat us, and made yak taste—well, less like yak.

Or perhaps we subconsciously, and consciously, associate light with goodness because it illuminates and clarifies the world around us. For example, I love to work in my woodshop. But awhile back, I noticed I was constantly migrating to one end of the shop to work on various projects. Then it hit me. I had six lights in the ceiling, but they were not evenly spaced. Five were on the side of the garage I preferred, with only one on the other end. Sure, when the garage door was open and it was light outside, it was fine. But when night fell, it was difficult for me to work on the dim side of the garage. (When working with power tools and sharp blades, visual clarity is kind of important.)

Light allows us to see and understand the environment around us. This, in turn, can spawn feelings of peace, safety, and calm (assuming the light isn't revealing imminent dangers, like hordes of zombies lurching toward you). And, most important of all for my digits and limbs, light allows me to make accurate cuts on my table or band saw.

Keep in mind that some see beauty in darkness. It can eliminate distractions, allow one to meditate peacefully, and encourage restful sleep.

But psychologists will tell you that one of the most grueling conditions a person can be forced to tolerate is light deprivation.

Darkness is often used in captivity to break down someone's sense of self. Light deprivation causes a person to become exhausted, confused, and disoriented. They lose awareness of where they are and what is or is not lurking in the dark around them. If they get hit in darkness, they can never truly stop fearing when and where the next painful attack may be coming from.

So if we're talking about metaphors, it seems that this description of light deprivation aptly depicts what type of world we are plunging into if we continue to allow the lightless negativity (anger and incivility) to cast its shadow on the world.

Light (Positive Energy) Is Kryptonite to the Dark (Negative Energy)

Martin Luther King said, "Darkness cannot drive out darkness; only light can do that. Hate cannot drive out hate; only love can do that."[55]

Dr. King was assassinated more than fifty years ago, yet hatred and prejudice are still very much alive and well today.

Dr. King eloquently and accurately captures a simple truth about the universe and the human heart. Darkness cannot reverse, diminish, or stop darkness. The only thing that can do that is light.

As we looked at different examples in previous chapters (I am thinking specifically of Yoko), the correlation isn't exact. Hate is not exactly equal to the absence of love. Still, for the purpose of this book, Dr. King's premise is right on.

For some of us, the ability to feel love for those we don't like is instant, like turning on all the lights in my workshop. In reality, that's probably the exception. For most of us, finding love for our enemies happens gradually.

We all have people we consider our enemies in some way—and we are all considered the enemy by someone. We perceive others as being clouded by darkness and negativity—but we may be perceived in the same way by our enemies. Whether we're trying to improve ourselves and replace negativity with light, or we're patiently trying to be the light that helps others emerge from cloudy darkness, it can be a frustrating, somewhat painful process.

Just as any change tends to be.

Despite the polarization we are witnessing in the world right now, I believe one message Dr. King was trying to teach us is that we can control our emotions of both love and hate. Every moment we breathe, we decide which emotion we will feed: the hate or the love.

Regardless of your race, economic status, age, sexual orientation, or political leanings, it's possible for you to love, forgive, and respect others—even in an often chaotic, hate-filled world where people constantly attack each other.

Be the Light That Ignites Other Lights—And Banish the Dark

Ultimately, hate will grow if left unchecked. King, Gandhi, Mandela, and others taught what I think is the best and purest approach to checking the spread of darkness.

While no process is guaranteed or void of hazard, the most effective approach I have witnessed or experienced is banishing hate with love. And if we are going to spread the light, we must first have the light.

I think back to my I-15 story in which the frightened husband was trying to reach his hospitalized wife. Was I bringing light and love to the situation? Hell, no. I was doing everything wrong and relying on instant certainty to create a perspective that was so far off base it was crazy. That tragically distorted perspective allowed me to fill my heart with justification, jealousy, anger, and contempt—all precursors to hate. I was not bringing the love. I cringe to think what a mess I would have made had the unknown 911 caller behind me not summoned law enforcement. I could have been the reason the young father didn't make it to the hospital in time to be with his wife and child in time. Ugh!

Bringing the love (i.e., light, positive energy) to a confrontation, no matter its size, is not easy—even if the confrontation is merely in your own mind as you get riled up about people you don't like, are irritated by, think are wrong, or really despise.

If we don't actively foster love in our thoughts and actions, its absence can create a vacuum that allows the darkness to take over. Your heart and mind are like rooms, and just as with any room, if you shut the blinds and turn off the lights, darkness fills the space.

If you do nothing—if you don't strive for tolerance, peace, and love—the darkness will take seed, spread its roots, and threaten to consume your heart.

Unlike the weeds of anger, distrust, and hate, the flowers of kindness, goodwill, trust, and peace have to be nurtured and tended.

Bringing love to a situation, whether in your thoughts or in person, doesn't mean you believe what your opponent believes, and it doesn't mean you like the person who harbors negative feelings toward you. It merely means you consider those who harbor anger and fuel negativity to be human. They are people. They're more important than their hate.

It means we may often disagree with others but their humanity is far more important than their message.

If you attack hate with hate, the world will not be a better place. What little satisfaction you gain will be fleeting at best and eventually to the detriment of everyone. A vengeful solution to a permanent problem is temporary and will do nothing but leave you feeling empty. Do you really want to leave a legacy of more hate for following generations?

Light, Dark, and Civility Today

Some no longer see political opponents as merely misguided or wrong; they perceive their political foes as evil, dangerous, and a threat to all we hold dear.

What's more, in our polarized "us versus them" world, we have groups and subgroups and sub-subgroups of people who see large swaths of humanity as enemies or foes. The polarized extremes of these groups dictate that the only way to deal with foes is to cancel them. Crush them. Eliminate them.

Vicious language often becomes vicious action, as it did in the case of Jeff, who got thrown off the plane when he started throwing punches. And that is the result of dehumanizing our foes. Once we begin to dehumanize those on the other side, it's a savage path leading to hate, contempt, and more violence.

Striving to end this cycle should be a goal and practice of every person who aspires to live by the Ruby Rule. We should rethink how we deal with conflict and foster more open, candid conversations.

We shouldn't fear disagreement; a free and just civilization relies on it. We have differences; we always have and hopefully always will. Differences should not be ignored and erased.

I propose we start by remembering our commonalities. We are all humans worthy of dignity and respect.

Are you shocked or offended by someone else's opinion? Take a breath, count to ten, and remember they have a right to that opinion. You do not have to compromise your values to listen authentically.

It's time we up our listening skills and really communicate. Let's use conflict to compromise and grow rather than demonize and destroy. Let's each of us foster peace instead of violence and work together to advance humanity.

When you demonize the other side, there can be no peaceful resolution.

Rewriting the Hate Script

Hate is kept alive only if we act our part in the hate script. But what if we altered that script? What if we all thumbed our noses at hate and chose not to play our part? The most upsetting thing we can do to mess up hate is to shine a light of love, forgiveness, tolerance, and compassion into the dark corners of hate, aggression, intolerance, and incivility. That will blow the ugly hate narrative apart and rewrite the script.

Remember, every person on the planet possesses the ability to be a light in the darkness. My good friend Dr. Paul Jenkins often talks about the nature of light and what happens when it comes up against darkness.

If I turn on my flashlight in a lightless, subterranean chamber, a beam of brightness cuts through the darkness like a lightsaber. I can point it anywhere in the cave and instantly illuminate that area.

But what about its counterpart? Is there such a thing as a "flashdark"? Fortunately, there is no tool I can turn on to shoot a beam of darkness through light or create a spot of darkness in a well-lit space. I mean, who would want to promote and amplify darkness?

The power of light—the positive energy we nurture and emit—can help make a difference in overcoming the tide of darkness and negative energy.

"When I despair," Gandhi said, "I remember that through history, the way of truth and love has always won. There have been tyrants and murderers, and for a time, they seem invincible, but in the end, they always fall—think of it—always."

Evil will always exist. The truth is, no amount of effort will eliminate evil. All we can do is focus on ourselves. Are we contributing to a more tolerant, loving humanity, or are we making things worse?

There will always be those selfish narcissists who lie to your face while stabbing you in the back. There will always be keyboard trolls who want to hate. There will always be crime, and innocent people will always have bad things happen to them.

But just because evil will always exist, don't stop trying to be a force for spreading good and civility. You might be tempted to think your kindness can't possibly make a difference in this world.

It can.

And you may be tempted to think you get a free pass to get angry and stoop to the level of those who speak and act in ways that fuel negative energy.

You don't.

Decency matters. Kindness matters. Goodness matters. Civility matters. Patience matters. Tolerance matters. Love matters. Be the change, lead by example, and let the ugly people, selfish liars, social media trolls, and haters self-destruct—because they will. That much is certain.

We don't have to be perfect about it. Just like we all have ups and downs, no one can live in the light all the time. The earth itself must go from light to dark about every twelve hours. As humans, we will feel pain, anger, frustration, and jealousy. The trick is to not give those emotions much attention. We all experience good and bad, joy and pain, fulfillment and regret, cruelty and kindness.

Don't get stuck in the churn of harmful, negative energy. Focus instead on the positive.

People who do bad things will always exist. But this book is for you, not them.

You have no real control over other people. You can't force someone to abandon the darkness for the light. I discovered this while driving at night with my lights off as everyone was trying to get my attention to help me. But my mind was made up. Thankfully, my wife's rational, sweet voice broke through (barely) my obstinance and helped me realize I was the one in the dark.

Love is the light that can reach someone huddled in the darkness. Years ago, I heard a story at a conference, though I don't know its origin. It tells of a five-year-old boy who was visiting his aunt and uncle in their new home. Early in the evening, he dozed off in a bedroom, and the kindly aunt covered him with a blanket and shut the door, thinking he might sleep through the night.

In the middle of the night, after everyone had gone to bed, the boy awoke, disoriented and afraid. He cried out in the darkness, "Aunt Nina!"

The aunt heard him from her bedroom across the hall. Groggy, she called back to her nephew as she tried to disentangle herself from her sheets so she could go to him.

"Aunt Nina, keep talking to me!" the boy cried. "I'm scared."

The aunt stumbled as she tripped on the rug, delaying her ability to reach the scared boy. "Okay!" she yelled back to him. "I'll be there in a few seconds. Why do you want me to keep talking? You can't even see me."

"When I can hear your voice, it gets light."

This boy was frightened by the darkness, which was compounded at first by the absence of somebody he loved. What he needed to feel secure was the reassurance of a loved one.

We all need to feel the love of those around us; it's essential to our self-confidence and safety. Those entrenched in the darkness of negativity can only be reached through acts and words of kindness, love, patience, and understanding.

No matter how many times we stumble and mess it up, the journey is worth the effort. Even if it simply decreases the hate on the planet by a little in one person, it will have proven valuable to all humanity—and not least of all, yourself.

When we are the beneficiaries of someone who has inspired us to be a light, we can be benefactors to those who desperately need to be a light themselves, regardless of whether they realize it. It's the ultimate Ruby Rule move.

If you, like Dr. King, can live this way and motivate others through your actions, you will have accomplished far more than most. You will have lived with light and love, and you will have helped others recognize the value of it. And that is truly a life well loved, well lived, and well lit.

Chapter Recap

- Many live in the darkness and instant certainty of hate, anger, hostility, and incivility—and don't even know it.

- The light of positive energy is more powerful than the darkness of negative energy.

- Love is more powerful than hate.

- Every day, everyone has a choice to make: feed the love or feed the hate.

- If we don't actively foster love in our thoughts and actions, its absence creates a vacuum that allows the darkness to take over.

- We may often disagree with others, but their humanity is far more important than their message.

- Since moving from hate to forgiveness, love, and empathy is a gradual process for many, lean into love and keep learning.

- Negativity, jealousy, distrust, and hate are your default unless you mindfully cultivate thoughts of positivity, care, trust, and love.

- Decency matters. Kindness matters. Goodness matters. Civility matters. Patience matters. Tolerance matters. Love matters. Be the change and lead by example.

Pause and Think

- Are you driving with your lights off? Could you be perpetuating hurtful, hateful ideas without even knowing it?

- As you plan your next day, brainstorm three ways you can feed the light and love in your thoughts and actions and starve the negative energy.

- Once you feel you've been successful in that, set a goal to conscientiously practice three things to feed the light each day for an entire week.

- Report to someone—or yourself in your journal—what you learned from this experiment.

CHAPTER 8

I FOUND THE AILING PUBLIC SQUARE IN THE HOSPITAL WAITING ROOM

A Plea to the Silent Majority to Make Their Voices Heard

A few years ago, I was at the hospital as my wife underwent an in-and-out, low-risk surgery.

I sat in a waiting room full of strangers with whom I had something in common. We all had loved ones in surgery.

Those who know me won't be surprised to find out that I struck up a conversation.

My conversation that day was sparked by the TV playing in the waiting room. The local news ran a clip about the volatile political divide in our nation. I wanted to know what people thought about the tension tugging at the seams of the country. It was, I admit, a rather strange thing for me to start talking about. The rules of polite conversation today have evolved to DON'T SPEAK ABOUT POLITICS, SOCIAL STANCES, OR ANY TOPIC THAT MAY INFURIATE ONE SIDE OR THE OTHER—WHICH COULD LEAD TO RAMIFICATIONS ON SOCIAL MEDIA.

Still, I was motivated to tactfully open a can of worms because I was writing this book and my mind was wrapped around these very issues. Besides, I have never been one to let some of the more nonsensical social mores get in the way, especially in hospital waiting rooms.

We began chatting about the political divide and the conflict it fuels. I must admit, I was a bit wary—not knowing what Pandora's box I had opened. Would our little microcosm of America replicate the tensions, anger, and intolerance seen in much of the macrocosm? Would our impromptu town-hall meeting turn ugly? After all, we were twelve strangers sitting around and chatting about hot topics like immigration, white privilege, BLM, climate change, guns, and LGBTQ rights. Would yelling commence, fists fly, and cops in riot gear swarm the room?

Curious how it turned out? You'll find out soon.

The New Code of Silence

My impromptu town hall in the hospital goes against the grain of current trends in the U.S. People today don't often engage in such meaningful conversations with their fellow citizens. Instead, they practice a form of self-censorship.

Naturally, we should distinguish between positive, Ruby Rule-based silence (motivated by tact, kindness, empathy, and sensitive civility) versus negative silence (motivated by anxiety, apprehension, and fear). There's a big difference. What the high levels of self-censorship in America reflect is primarily the latter, I believe.

According to a 2020 study by the CATO Institute, "Nearly two-thirds—62 percent—of Americans say the political climate these days prevents them from saying things they believe because others might find them offensive."

In our everyday lives, most are censoring what they say to conform to social norms. So, for example, if you hold an unpopular view, you are unlikely to share it with people you don't trust. But this is not what I mean by self-censorship. That falls under the category of social filtering. We all practice this from time to time—and thank heavens we do. The danger is when your social filter slowly expands, covering more and more issues, escalating your self-censorship and silencing your speech and public participation on important issues.

So what does it say about our culture when almost two-thirds of the population keep their thoughts mum? I suspect we stay silent because we're afraid our thoughts will be turned against us.

Because of our increasing polarization, many distrust each other and even detest their neighbors', family members', and coworkers' views and ideals. They suspect that sharing their beliefs publicly offers little or no reward. The reality is very different. But many people also recognize the risks in sharing their opinions. They believe that participating in public discourse and expressing their true opinion will cost them. Many fear that sharing unpopular opinions will compromise and even destroy their relationships with those they love and trust. Some are even fearful their very livelihood is on the line.

Free speech is not and has not ever been free, yet the price of such speech today has gone through the roof.

And this is a huge problem. Because the trademark and sure sign of a truly free and healthy society is that all people are encouraged to openly share their opinions and preferences, even if the government or the majority doesn't like them. And that means any of us should feel free to criticize, march, protest, scream, and even—I know this seems a foreign concept today—genuinely listen to others' opinions. This dialogue is essential if our freedoms are to be maintained. It requires a Ruby-Rule mindset. In a free-speech context, that looks like a willingness to respectfully listen to opposing views (treat others how they wish to be treated) and not react to angry rhetoric with anger. Instead, angry rhetoric should be met with calm, peace, empathy, and a shoe-shifting effort to understand. This entails anticipating and treating a person in a way they want to be treated, even though they're not yet aware of it; they may think they want to pick a fight and stir up a heated argument, but, really, they likely want to feel respected and heard.

This type of Ruby-Rule-infused environment would go a long way toward restoring the health and vigor of public debate and give us the confidence to voice our opinions without fear of reprisal.

The fact that more than six in ten Americans do not feel comfortable expressing their views should sound loud warning sirens in your mind. It's a sign of the rise—and settling in—of an orthodoxy-oriented culture characterized by a false sense of and certainty about truth and intolerance for those who dare to challenge that truth.

Most centrists (liberal, conservative, and independent) self-censor, while the extreme left and right have no problem voicing their opinions without fear of offending anyone . . . and, in fact, in many instances, are *trying* to offend someone.

Hence, if you are not on the fanatic fringe, you self-censor because the fringe will call you out and tell you that you are not liberal or conservative enough. And then you find your-self swimming in dangerous, cancel-infested waters, which is exactly where ESPN anchor Sage Steele found herself in 2020.

Not Authentic Enough

Steele, an African American, claims that her fellow Black jour-nalists at the network worked to get her kicked off an ESPN special about Black athletes' experience with injustice.

The reason?

She had apparently said and done some things that made her, according to other Blacks, not Black enough. Not an authentic voice of the Black experience. According to Joe Flint of the *Wall Street Journal*:

> Ms. Steele said colleagues told her she was considered for the special by the executive in charge, Michael Fountain, until two of the other on-air personalities involved, Elle Duncan and Michael Eaves, complained, saying Ms. Steele wouldn't be accepted by what they considered the Black community, according to the person familiar with her account to management.[56]

A few of the infractions that tarnished her authenticity in the eyes of some African Americans were that she:

1. Criticized Colin Kaepernick for kneeling during the National Anthem;
2. Declared herself a "proud bi-racial woman" (of a Black father and white mother)
3. Allowed a white studio guest to touch her hair

In the dust-up after Steele revealed that she had been "voted off the island," so to speak, some on Black Twitter attacked her.

Film producer and social media personality Tariq Nasheed tweeted, "Why in the hell would anyone take Sage Steele seriously on any issues pertaining to Black society?"[57]

Someone who goes by the handle Left Ph.D. tweeted, "Are we talking about this Sage Steele? Is this the same person who feels like her Black colleagues don't rock with her? Would you blame them for having an "All skinfolk ain't kinfolk" way of dealing with her?"[58]

In response to this vehement canceling of Steele, she provided a compelling argument:

Instead of praising or uplifting each other, way too many people of color choose to tear down, mock and spew hatred at other blacks who feel differently, think differently, or make decisions that are different from theirs. That, my friends, is hypocrisy at its best. Or should I say, its hypocrisy at its worst.

You don't get a hall-pass just because you're a minority. Racism is racism, no matter what color your skin is. So when you call me a sell-out, or a coon, or an Uncle Tom, or any other derogatory term to let me know that you disagree with me, you lose every ounce of credibility with those whom you deem racist at the drop of a hat.[59]

While some of what she says is very specific to her situation with the Black community, some of it can apply to our discussion of why Americans self-censor so much. As we have discussed, there are those who on social media and in their personal encounters "choose to tear down, mock and spew hatred at [others] who feel differently, think differently, or make decisions that are different from theirs."

And when that happens, as Steele found out, real-world consequences often follow.

The strength and engine of a healthy democracy is debate in good faith among opposing viewpoints with the goal of coming to a common ground that yields positive change and promotes the good of the people as much as possible.

And with the silent, moderate majority keeping silent out of fear—and with the outspoken extremes and intransigent tribes refusing to listen to any who disagree with them (and even attacking and canceling those who disagree with them)—powerful, corrosive forces erode the foundations upon which our society stands.

Speak Up, Speak Out, and Be Surprised

While it may seem that our differences are not only insurmountable but that trying to discuss or debate them may spark unpleasant—and possibly damaging—repercussions, it seems that a silent, "exhausted" majority of us are on the same page. But we don't know it because the extremists on each side domineer the airspace and can commandeer small armies of terror trolls to tweet-beat into cancelation those who dare to express a different opinion—all of which causes the moderate middle to clam up and stay out of the fray.

But recent surveys suggest that while the far right and far left might scream the loudest, they are vastly outnumbered by the reasonable citizens of the middle.

A 2018 study by the group More in Common acknowledges that "productive national dialogue about . . . critical issues has reached an impasse, in large part due to the widening gap between the major ideological and partisan perspectives."[60] And John Shattuck, a senior fellow at the Harvard Kennedy School Carr Center for Human Rights, confirms that "polarization is pushed by the political extremes."[61]

Several studies, however, seem to reveal the presence of a sleeping giant in American political and civic life. That sleeping giant is the very sane, very reasonable, very amenable-to-debate-and-compromise citizens of the middle—all of whom are exhausted by the drama and tension foisted upon us by our political "leaders" and their extremist minions.

The 2018 study by More in Common showed that 77 percent of Americans "believe our differences are not so great that we cannot come together."[62]

Those numbers appear to hold relatively constant, even at the time of this writing.

For example, Shattuck has overseen many surveys and reports that "affirm the strong presence of a middle ground in American politics."[63] He cites data from those studies showing that of the adults surveyed across America, 71 percent believe Americans "have more in common with each other than many people think." That total includes Republicans (78 percent), Democrats (74 percent), and Independents (66 percent).[64]

Many other studies confirm that most Americans can agree on common-ground outcomes that are good for all Americans. For example, one study asked respondents to rate twenty ideas "for building a more perfect union" on a scale of one to ten, with ten indicating strong agreement. The top ideas, which scored high across party and demographic lines (in other words, the silent, "exhausted" center), were the following:

- "We need to clean up all levels of government to make sure politicians are paying attention to the needs of American voters and not just corporations, campaign donors, and the wealthiest few." (8.4 average)

- "Americans need to spend less time fighting one another on social media and in politics." (8.3 average)

- "If America is to succeed going forward, we need to ensure that everyone, regardless of race, ethnicity, gender, or religious background, enjoys full legal equality and has a fair shot at economic success." (7.9 average)[65]

Those are encouraging numbers. And many feel that way when responding to a survey, but when they get into a face-to-face conversation or Twitter or Facebook exchange, they feel and act differently.

Would my impromptu town-hall meeting in the hospital bear out the results of all these surveys?

Stuck in the Middle with You

All of us in the waiting room were together for a few hours, and our conversation covered much ground. You could tell by the positions people took and the questions and answers they gave that we had Democrats, Republicans, and the rest somewhere on the spectrum between the two.

While we had differences on many subjects, we all agreed that our differences were not so significant that we couldn't all work together to make progress.

As I sat there, I could not help but feel grateful that others like me had opinions and were willing to politely—civilly—listen to the views of those with whom they disagreed. None in this group demonized or demeaned me when my opinion was contrary to theirs. And, in fact, by allowing each other to express our differences, we quickly found large swaths of common ground where we agreed on many things.

As far as I could tell, everyone in the room expressed disgust at the way many of our leaders and politicians behaved.

And the more we talked, the more our attitudes and actions synced with the results of all these studies showing there's a huge population of middle-of-the-ground citizens who agree on much and are willing to work with those who disagree with them.

I talk to many on this issue of anger and polarization in our society (it has preoccupied my thoughts lately). So many feel like they are strangers in their own country because of all the unsettling changes in society and the economy. The old certainties of the past are gone. These days, the idea of a secure job and the safety of a community where people knew one another and looked after one another seem like they are from a bygone era.

Some in our little group expressed uncertainty about who or what they could trust. They no longer could trust the institutions (church, law enforcement, major news organizations, politicians, and others) that once held us together. Everybody seems to have their own view of the world, making it harder to discern fact from fiction.

We, the people of the hospital waiting room, all agreed that certain news sources often echo the opinions of only one extreme or the other and that anyone who posted opposing views on social media was often attacked by angry, trolling mobs.

We all felt we are being encouraged to view each other as enemies and threats, not as fellow Americans with different experiences and viewpoints.

Some felt their only choice was to tune entirely out, while others could hear only the most extreme voices. Finally, one elderly woman in the group asked a rhetorical question: "Who is speaking for those of us who want the anger to stop? Who is speaking for those who believe in decency, equality, and tolerance?"

At this, her son poked her in the ribs and said, "Just tune in to Fox News, MSNBC, or CNN; according to them, they're our champions. They wouldn't lie to us." His quick wit and the sarcastic look on his face made us chuckle.

None of us felt like we could or should simply give up on forging a more unified country, but we all agreed we felt more fragmented and fractured than ever. The angry, loud fringes on the left and right were driving us from what we all wanted and were truly thirsty for 1) leaders more focused on finding common ground than pandering to their political bases to stay in power, and 2) a louder voice and greater influence on the national psyche from the moderate middle.

We all agreed on the concept articulated by Larry Kramer of the Hewlett Foundation: "There is no contradiction or incompatibility between caring passionately about an issue and taking the time to understand an opposing argument."[66]

But people can't communicate with each other if they don't get along or remain silent amid the noise.

Now, I know this impromptu town hall is anecdotal evidence rather than hard science, but our conversation was an encouraging sign amid all the incivility making headlines. It was a flicker of light in the gloom.

Taking Back the Public Square

My experience with my fellow citizens in the hospital waiting room gave me hope for the future of civility and our way of life. It made me feel an even more heightened sense of urgency to counter the extremism that drowns debate and drives policy.

Most citizens in the country are not out for blood. The majority (left or right) are moderates who want to talk. They want to listen. They still believe in civil dialogue and a free public square.

However, the screaming fanatics are driving the "exhausted majority" to silence on many issues. If you are a moderate liberal, you will be screamed at by fanatic liberals accusing you of not being liberal enough. If you are a moderate conservative, you will get similar treatment. So you stay quiet to avoid being attacked.

The fanatic fringes hijacking our public square and creating an ever-increasing division in society are endangering the foundation our Founding Fathers built for us.

In his essay, Kramer writes:

> Unless we can hear our opponents and make them feel heard (and they us), we stand little chance of maintaining our democracy. . . . We live at a time when many of our most cherished values are under attack or eroding (a painful reality highlighted by just how tired and banal that observation sounds). Among the most endangered ideals are a cluster

of principles associated with the Enlightenment philosophy that inspired the founding of our nation and have exemplified it at its best: toleration, rationality, freedom of conscience and the free exchange of ideas, belief in empiricism and reason. Central to these principles, and to the process of rational argument itself, is the idea of skepticism—skepticism about our own self-evident truths most of all.[67]

It's Time to Change the Tone

In 2012, the late Rush Limbaugh publicly called a Georgetown student of law a slut and prostitute for testifying in Congress in support of the Obama administration's mandate that employers include contraception in their plans.

Following a significant public outcry, Limbaugh was forced to issue an apology. Unfortunately, though, Limbaugh received more than just a few "amens" from those who believed someone having an opinion more liberal than their own justified their open defamation of the young woman.

Perhaps I expect too much, but aren't we entitled to better public discourse?

It has been challenging to define the boundary between the individual right to free will and civic responsibility. Unfortunately, it doesn't help us work through the problems when pundits resort to name-calling and turning complex issues into social media sound bites.

I bring up the Limbaugh story not to debate sexual freedoms and moral values. I am also not citing this story to discuss theocracy and liberty. This story is about how we as a society must learn to get along with one another and communicate our views of morality in a constructive, empathetic way. Although it can be difficult to talk about complex emotional issues, it is essential for a healthy, ethical, free, democratic society.

We must learn to have civil conversations about polarizing issues. Civility is the ability to have a conversation with others with whom you disagree. This ability to have an open, honest, free exchange of polarized messages without demonizing the messenger is vital to our humanity.

Public discourse on many emotional issues has become vulgar, mean-spirited, and laced with disdain for the other side.

It isn't easy to commit to civility. Conflict and disagreement will not disappear if we practice civil conversation, but civility is a better way to find common ground and explore differences.

It is time to change the tone of our conversations with the other side. And as we established in the previous section, we must change the tone by starting with ourselves and our own discourse.

What can we do to turn the tide of extremist ideologies and negative energy polluting our democracy? I'll touch on that a bit in the next chapter. I believe we need to practice something I call "civil restraint."

In the meantime, if you find yourself in a hospital waiting room, and you get the crazy urge to strike up a civil, Ruby-Rule-based conversation about hot-topic social issues, go ahead and venture into that uncertain space. You just might find the long-missing public square where civil speech is welcome, the free exchange of ideas is encouraged, and caring passionately about an issue doesn't preclude one from taking the time to understand an opposing argument.

Chapter Recap

- The majority (nearly two-thirds) of Americans self-censor opinions out of fear.

- We live in a society where voicing an opinion can adversely affect your ability to make a living.

- The self-censoring of the moderate middle emboldens the fanatical fringes so that they appear and sound louder than they really are. This feedback loop amplifies the extreme voices, leading to louder and more fanatical rhetoric and behavior.

- The truth is that most Americans can agree on common-ground outcomes that are good for all Americans—but only if we speak up and, more importantly, listen up.

- It is possible to care passionately about an issue and also take the time to understand an opposing argument.

Pause and Think

- Look for opportunities to invoke your own impromptu town-hall meeting. Make sure you provide a calm and reassuring voice that sets a positive tone for the group. If you've experienced such an opportunity, how did it turn out? What are your feelings as you consider what happened?

- Have you ever found yourself withholding an opinion out of fear? When this happens, take a moment and ask why. What will happen if you tactfully share your thoughts when you know those thoughts are not compatible with the thoughts of the majority you are with?

- Do you have a friend who thinks differently from you on a hot social topic? Is it possible to strike up a conversation not with the purpose of convincing them to side with you but rather to better understand their views? Try it and see what happens.

CHAPTER 9

ENTER THE VAULT

Creating a Psychological Safe Place for Civil Discourse

I would normally start the chapter with an experience from my life to set the stage for the concepts I want to explore.

But not this time.

I can't.

You see, I'm contractually bound to not share a personal story related to this concept. In a way, I've signed a nondisclosure agreement.

But that's okay. The interesting part of this nonstory, in fact, is what I *can't* tell you.

Before I share this concept, let me sketch the thought trail that led to it.

I was wondering what kind of framework we, as a society and as individuals, could put into practice to help us communicate civilly on a more consistent basis and perhaps pull us from the edge of the precipice that plunges into the destructive darkness of anger, rage, and venomous words and actions.

And as I pondered this, I thought of the Vault.

No, not the gymnastic event. Not Fort Knox.

This is something between my kids and me.

Welcome to the Vault

The Vault is a simple technique I use to create a safe space for
me and my kids to talk about sensitive, heated, awkward, or
embarrassing issues. It is a head and heart space we get into
when we have differences of opinion and want to speak can-
didly—and know that our frank comments will be kept private,
sacred, and never used against us in the future. It is a common
ground that allows us to freely express opinions without fear of
judgment, shame, rebuttal, or ridicule.

If one of my children and I are talking and the topic becomes
Vault-worthy, either of us can invoke it by saying, "Vault."

My kids know I take this very seriously, and I know they
do as well. Once the Vault is invoked, we both enter a mental
and emotional space that is uniquely ours and ours alone. It is
a space where we feel at peace because we know that whatever
is said is locked away. Blood pressure drops, intonation softens,
emotions are pacified, and we focus intently on listening to what
the other has to say.

No matter the topic, no matter the emotional energy, what
we say remains locked in a vault of trust. My kids know I will not
be sharing what they say with their siblings, mother, spiritual
leader, friends, readers of this book. No one.

My kids and I have had conversations in the Vault about
many delicate and complicated subjects—all heavy issues kids
face today and may be afraid to talk to their parents about. And
we have used the Vault to resolve disagreements about haircuts,
homework, and housework; to express opinions on religion and
politics; to iron out misunderstandings and resolve frustrations.
We have talked about pornography, cheating in school, LGBTQ,
abortion, premarital sex, depression, drug use, taxes, war, eating
disorders, and more. We've discussed important topics I would
never have raised with my parents.

It doesn't matter if I had the conversation with them when they were toddlers or in their thirties. It's in the Vault. It's like our conversations have attorney-client privilege. And that opens the door for the candid, open exchange of opinions and ideas without either side fearing retribution, hostility, canceling, or judgment.

It turns out, research backs me up on the concept of the Vault.

At Google headquarters, they wanted to know what makes a successful team. They found five key dynamics that set successful teams apart from others. First on their list was psychological safety. In other words, "Can we take risks on this team without feeling insecure or embarrassed?"[68]

In other words, can you open up and be vulnerable without feeling like you'll get in trouble or be mocked or negatively perceived? It sounds an awful lot like the Vault.

Here's what Google researchers had to say:

Psychological safety was far and away the most important of the five dynamics we found—it's the underpinning of the other four. How could that be? Taking a risk around your team members seems simple. But remember the last time you were working on a project. Did you feel like you could ask what the goal was without the risk of sounding like you're the only one out of the loop? Or did you opt for continuing without clarifying anything, in order to avoid being perceived as someone who is unaware?

Turns out, we're all reluctant to engage in behaviors that could negatively influence how others perceive our competence, awareness, and positivity. Although this kind of self-protection is a natural strategy in the workplace, it is detrimental to effective teamwork. On the flip side, **the safer team members feel with one another, the more likely they are to admit mistakes, to partner,**

and to take on new roles. And it affects pretty much every important dimension we look at for employees. Individuals on teams with higher psychological safety are less likely to leave Google, they're **more likely to harness the power of diverse ideas from their teammates,** they bring in more revenue, and they're **rated as effective twice as often** by executives.[69]

I added the bold for emphasis on certain benefits I feel my kids and I have enjoyed from our vault. We feel safer, which makes us more likely to open up—even if what we have to share is negative or embarrassing. We might adopt diverse advice or ideas from each other. And it seems to make our relationships more effective at growing closer and becoming better.

The concept of the Vault is also relevant to the conditions needed to engage in civil discourse with our fellow Americans and human beings in this toxic crisis of civility. And providing one another a safe space to express opinions is a foundational idea of the Ruby Rule.

The Need for a Vault Space in Our Daily Dialogue

There are many reasons divisiveness, anger, and hostility in our communications and actions are prevailing over unity, calm, and civility. Let's look at a few.

Social Media Is Fertile Ground for Breeding Trolls

You say things online you would rarely utter in person. Why are we angrier and faster to torch others we disagree with online?

One reason is because in many instances, we're anonymous—either literally anonymous or typing at a person we don't know personally, so we're practically anonymous. Even with a real profile pic and username, we still don't have the connection online that we feel face-to-face. When there is no real connection and no consequences for boorish, rude, offensive, provocative communication, it's easier to belittle, bully, and crucify others.

The same phenomenon occurs with drivers in traffic. (Ahem. No comment from me about a certain driver of a pickup truck facing off against a certain Bronco . . .). Most drivers feel it's okay to be more aggressive in their cars. Occasionally, this phenomenon allows for cutting others off, not letting others merge, honking horns, making obscene gestures, tailgating, and yelling expletives out the window. Why? Because we're protected in a four-thousand-pound tank, and we see other vehicles—not other people. If someone's trying to merge, we don't see them as a young mother with a car full of kids; we see them as a vehicle causing us grief.

Similarly, when online, we can't see those on the other side. It's easy to be a big, fat jerky-face. We talk about how the internet connects us, and it does, but it also plays a dehumanizing role in our interactions with others.

Negative News Nets Big Ratings

Long ago, media moguls cracked the code: they figured out that bad news sells. Feeding our fears attracts audiences and boosts ratings.

Today, it's not just media moguls publishing the news; it's everybody. Facebook, Google, Tik-Tok, YouTube, and other social media firms use algorithms to intentionally spotlight the posts that get the most clicks—whether from a news outlet or an influencer or a Tweet trend. And videos and reports of incivility go viral more often than posts that are civil.

Our human nature is to go low, and in our society today, sadly, hate creates more clicks than love.

I've wrestled with this. I'm dedicated to making my books and posts places of hope, help, and encouragement. Yet, if I title posts positively, fewer read them than if I make the negative play.

When I write posts and thoughts, I try avoiding anger, hate, outrage, cynicism, and melodrama. I try to write positive pieces. Like in any sales pitch, I lead with the problem most people see; I define it and quickly move to suggesting possible solutions.

If you want to be known in our hyperfast media world today, sadly, pushing anger, hate, and division has a proven track record of attracting attention.

Negative Attention Is Better Than No Attention

Technology is creating a strange phenomenon. We've never been so connected—able to video call people in far-flung places on any continent, follow their lives in intimate detail on social media, chat with them as you play games together, and more. Paradoxically, the technology we use to connect has contributed to us feeling incredibly alone. Technology decreases our need and ability to have real conversations, real human connections, real intimacy.

While you may have hundreds or thousands of followers, it's likely you have fewer friends with whom you interact face-to-face. And often, when you feel alone or abandoned, you may feel the impulse to create a stir. Start some drama. Anything that puts you on others' radars and forces attention your way.

An unfriendly click, comment, or dislike can make you feel relevant, and relevance feels better than emptiness. Negative contact allows you to interact, as opposed to zero contact, which makes you feel like you don't exist. Thus, hostile interaction can feel better than no interaction.

I find that the angrier someone is, the lonelier they are. So when I see a person in an angry tirade, I assume they are a miserably lonely person crying out for attention, hoping to get noticed.

Be the one to reach out. Be the one to be kind. Especially when you disagree with others—and yes, it's possible to be kind to lonely trolls. This is part of the Ruby Rule approach—to treat the lonely how they want to be treated by giving them attention (Platinum Rule) but then leveling up and anticipating a need the troll may not even be aware of: kindness, patience, empathetic attention (Ruby Rule).

Information Overdose

Due to nonstop text, social media, and 24/7 news feeds, you have access to and must process more information than any human being who ever lived on this planet.

My parents and grandparents processed only the information they needed. They knew only so many people; when our neighbor was sick, they helped by mowing the lawn or bringing in a meal. News traveled at the speed of newspaper, radio, and gossip.

Now, hundreds of times a day, we get up-to-the-second details on pandemics, mass shootings, murders, abuses, violence, riots, plane crashes, tornadoes, global warming, and wars that kill thousands and even millions, but we rarely if ever know anyone involved and are unable to help except through giving a few dollars to some GoFundMe page. We're relentlessly choked with info we can't fully digest, let alone swallow.

What's that doing? Well, it makes us anxious and distrustful.

On top of the bad news, you see friends post about their lavish vacations, cars, or dinners, which breeds loneliness and envy, which leads to anger, anxiety, and depression.

The more we know, the more uneasy we become and the more we can be triggered into feeling angry and lashing out.

Creating a Vault Space for Our Conversations with Others

With more volatile communications and angrier people these days, is it possible to create a version of the Vault when you communicate with others—even when the people you're trying to communicate with are aggressive, hostile, negative, or otherwise soulless?

Listen, I don't have all the answers that might solve this problem. But the more I think about it, the more it seems like the Ruby Rule—which is the highest level of the Golden Rule continuum—offers a way to turn the tide against negativity one conversation at a time. That is something you have control over—and it can have a profound effect that diffuses hostility.

The following are some examples of what it looks like in action.

Sarah Silverman's Phantom Fender Bender

Comedian Sarah Silverman was out shopping in Hollywood. When she pulled into a parking space, a man got out of the car next to hers and started screaming at her.

"What's wrong with you? You hit my car, you bitch."

Here's the problem: Silverman was certain she hadn't come close to hitting the gentleman's car.

Journalist Geoff Edgers writes,

> Standing there, Silverman had a choice: shout back or try one of her social experiments. Could kindness convert this negative energy into something positive? "I'm so sorry," Silverman said without a tinge of sarcasm. "Show me where the scratch is. I'll pay for it." That's all it took. The man was disarmed. He told her to forget about it.[70]

I am deeply intrigued by this story. How many of us would have reacted the way she did in this situation?

As I read about the man's aggressive reaction, I can imagine myself meeting anger with rage, shouting louder, and issuing profanity with a Tarantino-worthy tirade of expletives. Any human would feel justified in doing this. We are being attacked. We didn't start this. An eye for an eye and a tooth for a tooth.

But in this powder keg of an encounter, Silverman apologized sincerely (though she knew she hadn't hit the car) and offered to pay for any damage.

Where on the Golden Rule continuum does Silverman's reaction fall?

Golden Rule: Treat others how *you* want to be treated.

In this case, I would want to be treated by being left alone and not confronted by a guy lying about hitting his car and calling me nasty names, so I might turn and walk away, avoiding confrontation. I mean, I'd have to; otherwise, I'd be provoked into slugging the guy.

Platinum Rule: Treat others how *they* want to be treated.

Perhaps the shouting man wanted a verbal fight. Maybe it's his thing—accusing people of fender benders and starting a ruckus. Who knows? But in a weird way, you could treat him Platinum-style and give him what he wants: an angry shouting match. He wants a chance to vent, release all the negative emotions he's feeling, and be seen and heard. Meeting anger with anger may give him that.

Ruby Rule: Treat others how they *really* want to be treated.

Silverman hit pause on any aggression or fear she might have felt. She seemed to project herself into the man confronting her. Perhaps he was having a rotten day. A rotten life. Maybe he felt alone and alienated. Perhaps over the years, these pent-up feelings built inside him until the pressure cooker could contain them no longer and he exploded. Perhaps like the Bronco driver on the shoulder of I-15 passing everyone, the man was dealing with direly ill loved ones. Whatever it was, Silverman didn't start with the assumption that the man was in the wrong or deserved anger in return. If she were having an unhinged day, she would likely want to be treated with compassion and patience. Like all of us. So she countered his rage by agreeing with him and using a kind, sincere, apologetic tone.

"I think people can be changed," Silverman says, "but they're never going to be changed by feeling judged."[71]

In essence, she created a Vault for her and her antagonist. She created a safe, judgment-free zone in which the angry man could deescalate.

And she did it again with one of her internet trolls.

In 2017, she wanted to connect with Trump supporters and engage them in civil dialogue. One Trump supporter, Jeremy Jamrozy from San Antonio, Texas, tweeted, calling her a c***.

It would be so easy for any human being attacked that way to become enraged and attack back. Or send his tweet to his work and get him fired. Or re-tweet it so it got picked up by news outlets and other groups who would publicly shame the man. That would have been karma coming back to bite him in the booty and could have been very satisfying.

Except, it's not the principle of the Ruby Rule. And it's not how Silverman handled the situation. What she did, I think, was extraordinary.

First, she scrolled through Jamrozy's online history. Then she tweeted him. And this is how she responded to someone who had just called her the *c* word: "I believe in you. I read ur timeline & I see what ur doing & your rage is thinly veiled pain. But u know that. I know this feeling. see what happens when u choose love. I see it in you."

Jamrozy apologized to her. He admitted that he had been molested while growing up. He said he felt alone.

Silverman continued the conversation with him: "Dood I don't care. I'm fine. I see something in you. My gut tells me you could have a great life. My shrink says we don't get what we want, we get what we think we deserve. I'm telling you, you deserve so much more than you know."

The two ended up meeting in person. She gave him a gift. He paid for her parking meter. "I haven't shaken someone's hand in a year," Silverman says, "but I gave him a big handshake. And I go, 'Look at us. We were arch enemies and now we're best friends.'"

Bill Donahue Tries to Talk to His Trolls Face-to-Face

In his article, "This Rural Liberal Set Out to Talk to His Pro-Trump Neighbors: It Didn't Go Well—Until It Did," Bill Donahue reports on his experiment in trying to have offline, civil conversations with his Facebook trolls.[72]

The story begins with Donahue, who lives in the small New Hampshire town of Gilmanton, posting a picture of a Black Lives Matter (BLM) sign in front of the town hall. He would be hosting a BLM rally in a few days on the town commons. It was June 2020.

"I knew that I was taking a controversial stance," Donahue says. "In Gilmanton, as of 2019, 96.5 percent of the residents were, like me, White. In November, 57 percent of the voters here chose to reelect Donald Trump. I was allying with the decentralized racial justice movement, which decries violence against Black people, because I wanted to suggest that, even in a tradition-bound small town, change is possible."

Predictably, after his Facebook post announcing the rally, more than three hundred comments—most of them vitriolic, demeaning, threatening, or all of the above—came in. In fact, due to the threats to Donahue and the Facebook-page monitor, his post was pulled.

Like Silverman, Donahue decided to try a social experiment in civility and civil dialogue, or, as I perceive it, he performed a Ruby Rule analysis.

He says, "I embarked on an experiment. I began approaching the myriad locals who, in writing, have attacked me and my political allies. I wanted to know whether liberals and conservatives can still even talk to each other in rural America, and I wondered: What if we took the dialogue offline?"

In November 2020, he began his quest.

"All told, I write to 13 detractors," he says. "They've shown great swagger on Facebook, but now they're ducking me, almost en masse. What's going on? To be fair, I'm more or less ambushing them. An average of 350 million photos go up on Facebook every day. They're public pronouncements, but almost none of them elicit a call from a journalist."

Eventually, Donahue was able to meet with sixty-five-year-old Rick Notkin, a retired nurse and gun advocate. The two met at a diner and engaged in civil conversation, exchanging differing viewpoints. "Our luncheon chat is doing what dialogue should do," Donahue says. "It's making me see my opponent as complex and human." (Note: This is a great example of shoe-shifting.)

Next, Donahue met with a retired Air Force staff sergeant. Valerie Cote, who spent sixteen years as an ironworker, responded to Donahue's request with: "Would not mind speaking about politics. Thank you for reaching out!"

Cote, whose front yard has a sign that reads: "If you can read this, you're in range!" invited Donahue into her home, where they shared cups of coffee and uninhibited, delightful conversation.

In other words, they entered the Vault.

The Vault offered such a place of trust and safety for these two politically diverse people that Cote's husband walked into the room after she and Donahue had been talking for two hours and said, "This is a great conversation."

"Great conversations," Donahue declares, "are rooted in courage and trust. We need them to keep our nation civil and stable."

Amen, brother.

But he continues: "And during the past few weeks I've seen just how difficult it is to make them [civil conversations] happen.

Over and over, I've been stonewalled and reminded that a lot of people would rather say cruel things online than talk in person."

Donahue concludes: "I settled in this little town in the hills six years ago guided by a belief in its friendly spirit, and even now, as our political divide hangs on, as fraught as ever . . . I can still see that friendly spirit glimmering at times. On the day after Cote and I meet, she will post a picture of us, masked, on Facebook along with a note celebrating the good questions asked on both sides. One of my critics, an arch right-winger who said no to an interview, will applaud in the comments section with an emoji of an American flag."

That, I believe, is the power of the Vault—a concept rooted firmly in the Ruby Rule.

Signs of Civility

In West Jordan, Utah, during the 2020 presidential election, two backyard neighbors turned out to be polar opposites. Robert Vest supported Donald Trump. Jerry Enright supported Joe Biden.

The neighbors had been friendly and chatted at the backyard fence many times, not knowing much about the other's political stance. Then, as the election drew close, they found themselves talking politics, and each was shocked to find out which candidate the other supported.

"Suddenly," wrote television news reporter Alex Cabrero, "the two neighbors found themselves in a situation that has torn many friendships apart."[73]

Instead of drawing apart, however, Enright and Vest grew closer. At a poignant moment in their relationship, they created a safe space to talk openly about their opinions without feeling judged.

Does that sound familiar?

That's the Vault. A safe space where trust can bloom.

Based on that safe space, Enright and Vest began having many civil, engaging political discussions. They still were friends—even though they disagreed about politics and policies. They practiced the Ruby Rule and respectfully disagreed while prioritizing friendship and empathy over uncompromising dogma and vicious verbal attacks.

"I'm not sure how to solve the world's problems, but I'm certainly not going to let all of this divisiveness come between me and him," Enright said.

"He means more to me than this fighting," said Vest.

So when both neighbors put up yard signs for their candidates, they decided to make a statement in favor of civility. In both yards, they put up Trump and Biden signs, and in between them, a third sign: "We disagree, but we still get along."

"We kind of did something good here," said Vest. "I'm concerned about the country. He's concerned about the country. We want the best for the country."

Cabrero concludes, "Even though both sides think their way is better, these two neighbors are proof the debate doesn't have to be filled with the kind of anger, hatred and vulgarity that seems to have become the norm on social media message boards. Both admit there are serious issues to talk about and it's not as easy as just talking. But they also say they understand talking is where we must start."

"I think our country is big enough and strong enough to get through it," Enright said.

"If you're just going to fight, you're not going to get anything accomplished," said Vest.

When the Color of a Ruby Is Black and White

If you haven't heard the story of Daryl Davis, it's fascinating. At the very least, you should check out his Ted Talk. But there are also tons of news stories, interviews, and even a documentary featuring Davis.

What makes him so noteworthy?

He is a Black musician who one day met a member of the Ku Klux Klan—and then became his friend.

It was 1983, and Davis was the pianist for a country-music band. He was the only person of color in the band, and their gig was in a bar well known as an unofficial whites-only bar.

On a break, a man came up to Davis, put his arm around him, and told him he'd never "heard a black man play as well as Jerry Lee Lewis."

The man bought Davis a drink and began talking about music and race. Then the man revealed he was a member of the local KKK and showed Davis his card.

What does the concept of the Vault teach us about a situation like this?

If ever there were a cauldron of hatred, hostility, and violence ready to boil over, this was it.

This, however, turned into a friendly meeting. And it led to the two men becoming friends. And having more conversations. And Davis meeting more Klan members. And having discussions with them.

What is it about Davis that allows him to successfully connect with members of the KKK, become their friend, and even be invited to weddings and become the godfather of some of their children?

"We have a conversation," Davis says. "We have civil discourse. I'm there to hear what their concerns are, what their fears are, what myths have set them off, and hopefully to dispel some of those fears."[74]

Davis finds common ground with those who embrace an ideology of hate. He does this on the premise that these are fellow

Americans and fellow human beings. He does a lot of listening and doesn't judge those with whom he speaks, even though they espouse abhorrent beliefs. He creates a Vault wherein both he and the members of the KKK with whom he speaks feel a sense of trust and safety in which they can speak what's on their minds.

And do you know what has happened as a result of this lifelong pursuit of civil conversation? He's been (directly) responsible for forty to sixty members and (indirectly) over two hundred people leaving the KKK.

"He found that the Klansmen had many misconceptions about blacks, which stem mostly from intense brainwashing in their youth. When they got to know him, it was more difficult to maintain their prejudices."[75]

Many civil rights groups have criticized Davis for even making the attempt to befriend the enemy. The goal, they say, should be to destroy the Klan.

Davis's response encapsulates what civil discourse between two parties with seemingly insurmountable viewpoints can look like.

"I'm not out to destroy individuals," he said. "I'd like to see them destroy their own ideology. When you seek to destroy somebody, all you do is empower them. These are my fellow Americans. These are my fellow human beings. I want them to see something and come to the realization: 'This is a better path for me, and I'm going to help get other people out of there.'"[76]

Failing to find common ground—to even make the effort—can short-circuit attempts at civility in conversation. "All too often," Davis says, "some people don't read the backstory and jump to a conclusion and that's where it stays. And the anger and the anxiety and venom and animus comes out."[77] Sounds like instant certainty to me.

And Davis subverts instant certainty on both sides with Ruby-Rule-rooted actions. He listens with respect and a humble desire to know what other people think. Then he takes it to a higher level and gives to the enemy something they didn't even know they wanted: friendship and brotherly love with someone they are supposedly supposed to hate. And it is only then that the foundations upon which a person's anger and hate are built begin to crumble.

Mr. Rogers Saves the Neighborhood

It was 1969. Two years had passed since the U.S. Congress approved federal funding for public television. But now that budget was under the scrutiny of Senator John Pastore, a Democrat from Rhode Island and chair of the United States Senate Subcommittee on Communications.

Known as gruff, impatient, and a critic of children watching too much television, Pastore was inclined to fulfill President Richard M. Nixon's desire to cut the $20 million grant for the Public Broadcasting Service (PBS) down to $10 million, which would lead to the demise of several educational programs for kids. In a public hearing before the committee, Pastore listened to various advocates for PBS who made a variety of arguments to convince the committee—and mainly Pastore—to approve the full funding.

It was clear to all that Pastore was against passing the full budget. What's more, he was impatient with many of the witnesses, especially when they read long, philosophical statements and cited scholarly research. He seemed a bit bored, perhaps, wanting to finish the hearing so he and his committee could complete the vote to cut PBS funding.

And so it was that the last witness to testify before the committee was a very young Fred Rogers, creator of *Mr. Rogers' Neighborhood*. The show was new—as new as the fledgling PBS—and Pastore didn't know Rogers or the show.

As Rogers began to testify, Pastore's interactions with Rogers sounded adversarial and curt.

But then something interesting happened.

They found common ground.

And upon that common ground, they built a Vault.

Both men cared deeply about children. More specifically, they cared about the media—positive and negative—consumed by children and how it affected those children.

The first move toward rapprochement came from Rogers. "I'm very much concerned, as I know you are, about what's being delivered to our children in this country."

Video of the exchange cuts back and forth between the faces of both Rogers and Pastore.[78] As Rogers utters this, Pastore's face seems to shift a bit. He appears less skeptical, subtly nodding in agreement with Rogers's statement about being concerned with what children watch.

Rogers continues describing his program and how it constructively and imaginatively helps children. Pastore asks, "How long a program is it?"

Pastore's body language was speaking volumes. He's now leaning forward thoughtfully, and as Rogers responds, Pastore nods almost approvingly. The look on his face shifts again; now he appears inquisitive and completely nonaggressive. Ever so subtly, something has changed.

Pastore quickly follows up, speaking to aides offscreen. "Can we get a copy of this so we can see it?" He turns back to Rogers and says, "Maybe not today, but I'd like to see the program."

Rogers continues. "This is what I give. I give an expression of care every day to each child. To help them realize that they are unique. I end the program by saying, 'You've made this day a special day by just you're being you. There's no person in the whole world just like you, and I like you just the way you are.'"

Pastore's face now looks pensive—almost as if he is beginning to change his mind about cutting the funding for PBS, which is impossible, of course, because Pastore is dead set on cutting the budget in half.

Rogers describes how he strives through his program to show children that feelings are "mentionable and manageable" and that if that message reaches the children in the audience, it will be a positive development for their mental health.

Pastore's response? He now says aloud what his body language said minutes previous. "Well, I'm supposed to be a pretty tough guy, and this is the first time I've had goosebumps for the last two days."

Rogers responds, confirming that he and Pastore are both on the same side and advocating for the same thing. "I'm grateful, not only for your goosebumps, but also your interest in our kind of communication." He pauses. "Could I tell you the words to one of the songs which I feel is very important?"

"Yes," Pastore says.

Rogers recited the song:

What do you do with the mad that you feel, when you feel so mad you could bite? When the whole wide world seems oh so wrong, and nothing you do seems very right. What do you do? Do you punch a bag? Do you pound some clay or some dough? Do you round up friends for a game of tag or see how fast you go? It's great to be able to stop when you've planned a thing that's wrong and be able to do something else instead and think this song. I can stop when I want to, can stop when I wish. Can stop-stop-stop anytime and what a good feeling to feel like this and know that the feeling is really mine. Know that there's something deep inside that helps us become what we can, for a girl can someday be a lady, and a boy can someday be a man.

Before Rogers can utter the last syllable, Pastore jumps in. "I think it's wonderful. I think it's wonderful." There's a dramatic pause, then Pastore finishes with, "Looks like you just earned the twenty million dollars."

Applause breaks out in the House chamber.

Common ground—and two people allowing each other to express their opinions respectfully—led to adversaries finding they were really allies all along. That is a perfect summation of what the Vault is and what it can do. And why it's a cornerstone concept of the Ruby Rule.

Common Denominators

What do these stories teach us about communicating civilly with those with whom we fundamentally disagree?

I believe these examples illustrate the need to practice the Ruby Rule, which is a prerequisite to creating a Vault for civil dialogue. Silverman meeting aggression with empathy and humility; Donahue engaging his trolls in person to better understand them; Enright and Vest talking and letting their neighbors know they could disagree and still be friends; Daryl Davis seeking to listen and understand, creating a safe space for open dialogue, and latching on to commonalities upon which to build a relationship; Mr. Rogers looking past the gruff exterior and skeptical nature of his seeming foe so that they could find common ground.

I have one final story that illustrates why finding common ground with someone you don't agree with, or don't even like, is the lynchpin to making progress toward civility in society today.

Finding Common Ground

Okay, I lied. I do have a personal story to tell in this chapter. However, it's not sealed in the Vault, so I'm cleared to share it.

While working in Europe, I was asked to set up a pan-European call center. We had more than six hundred employees taking calls for many large organizations across the continent. We hired employees from Holland, England, Italy, Spain, Germany, France, Russia, Norway, Denmark, Sweden, Belgium, Morocco, Ukraine, and Finland. We were doing technical support and customer service work in almost every European language for some of Europe's biggest telecommunications and technology firms.

For the most part, those I worked with were open-minded, kind, and tolerant individuals who got along. Did we have differences between employees? Sure, with that many people and cultural backgrounds, there were bound to be differences of opinion. Everyone had grown up with different traditions, histories, faiths, cultures, languages, customs, and perspectives.

Some differences were minor and insignificant; others seemed to touch a nerve that created a great deal of passion and sometimes pain. Like in the United States, politics and religion were two hot buttons that could generate some intense emotions.

Whenever I had a group that was struggling based on these differences, I did a simple team-building exercise with them. At lunch, I invited fifteen to twenty people into the training room. I paid for lunch. I never really told them why I invited them, but I always handpicked those who would attend.

Little did they know that at least half of those I'd invited were chosen because they were struggling to get along. I don't know if they felt it, but as the managing director, I sure did.

These lunches became a very big deal and coveted invite. I arranged the chairs in a circle. As the attendees came in, each found a seat.

It was clear who felt comfortable with whom.

I started with just a quick introduction to set the stage, and then we grabbed a bite to eat. I told them they were going to spend the hour telling stories, not listening to me telling stories to them. They all knew I was a big-time storyteller, but now they were going to tell stories to each other. This often had the attendees looking at each other in a bit of panicked confusion. Some asked, "What stories are we going to tell?" I coyly said, "You'll find out after lunch."

Lunch was easy finger food: typically pizza or sandwiches. There was chatting, laughing, and visiting for the next twenty minutes or so while everyone ate. But the interactions were almost always limited to those who felt comfortable with each other. When I stood back and quietly observed, I could quickly spot who was in and who was out. Some small groups were clustered and interacting, while others ate quietly by themselves. Perhaps they were shy, or maybe they were being naturally ostracized by the small cliques, but there were always those who were loners and not included.

I was pained to see the loners being casually shunned or ignored. Their feelings of loneliness were real and made my heart ache. I sometimes overheard them say they would rather be alone. They may have thought they wanted to be alone, but I believe we all crave human connection. We all want to be part of a tribe. We all want to feel accepted, safe, and valued. I have found this need for belonging to be universal. It is not contingent on race, age, faith, gender, wealth, or culture. Loneliness is loneliness no matter who you are, how old you are, or where you're from.

After about twenty minutes, we cleaned up and took our seats. I placed in the middle of the room a box filled with emotion-provoking storytelling prompts, such as "My first kiss," "An embarrassing moment in my life," "A moment my parent/s made me proud," "My first day of school," "A moment I felt I had no voice," and "My first crush."

I had everyone reach into the box and randomly pick a slip of paper. As they read the prompts, some instantly smiled, while others took a few minutes to ponder. But within a few minutes, their stories started flowing.

As they shared and listened to others share, they began to discover common ground they didn't know they had.

They began to build bonds of empathy for one another. During the next hour or so, they shared stories in which they talked about their fears, hopes, dreams, and positive and negative experiences with their job. As they did so, they began to realize they had far more in common than they first assumed. Having them open up in a safe, Vault-like place allowed their humanity to take center stage instead of race, citizenship, gender, political leanings, or faith.

What seemed like vastly different individuals who had nothing in common quickly became a group of coworkers with a lot in common. Many of the fears, hopes, and wishes of the middle-aged man from Russia were strikingly similar to those of the young lady from Belgium. When one person described the pain they felt when one of their parents passed away, others in the group who had shared that experience could instantly empathize and relate. Suddenly, some of the loners were not loners. Some of the culturally conditioned cliques and stereotypes faded just a bit.

It was fun for me to observe these same individuals at work weeks later. The impromptu lunch outings, smoking-room banter (yes, back in the '90s, many young Europeans smoked), and watercooler chatter was more inclusive, cross-cultural, and empathetic.

Opening up and telling their stories—and listening to the stories of others—allowed these radically different individuals to find common ground. It allowed them to focus on what they had in common instead of what their respective cultures had taught them about each other.

Wherever I go in this world, I realize people are pretty much the same, with the same hopes, fears, dreams, and desires. But our differences are more likely to be pointed out, talked about, feared, shamed, and attacked than our similarities are to be honored, embraced, and celebrated.

In the next chapter, we'll consider specific principles in communication that can help you find common ground with those who might disagree with you, those who seem alien and different, or those who are hostile to you.

Why reach out to them in civility? It's the Ruby Rule, my friends. And it seems to be the only way to begin uniting a divided, increasingly uncivil world.

Chapter Recap

- We need to create Vault space—a place of psychological safety—in our daily dialogue.

- The Vault is a core concept of the Ruby Rule and opens wide the door for civil dialogue to enter.

- When you find common ground, passionate differences seem to melt away, or, at the very least, the differences are not all that passionate and problematic. Common ground helps build bridges of understanding.

Pause and Think

- Have you ever been confronted with hostility? How did you respond? How did it turn out? What, if anything, would you have done differently?

- Challenge: The next time you're confronted with hostility in a conversation, try countering it with kindness and understanding, seeking to find some common ground.

- Do you know of a neighbor or workmate who is from a different country, speaks a different language, or has a different faith? Find a way to treat them to lunch, learn more about them, and discover why they are the way they are. Look for similarities, not differences.

CHAPTER 10

THE MUMMIFIED CHEERLEADER, THE TRANS-AM DUDE, AND CIVIL RESTRAINT

How to Practice Mental Jiujitsu

In the fall of 1976, I was a sophomore at Monta Vista High School in Cupertino, California. As a member of the wrestling team, I hit the weight room every morning from 6:00 a.m. to 7:00 a.m. We weren't the only sweaty athletes using the gym in the predawn hours that fall. Our water polo team did so as well.

I remember one Friday morning that bicentennial year. It was the day of the big football game against our archrivals, Cupertino High. As usual, our team and the water polo team were pumping iron. There was some definite sweaty-teen stench in the air.

About halfway through our workout, 6:30-ish or so, the wrestling coach strolled into the room. We were all focused on our reps, not on the mischievous grin on coach Ron Edwards's face—not until he spoke, almost nonchalantly saying, "You know, if this were *my* high school and the cheerleaders from the rival school were toilet-papering *my* rally court, *I* would do something about it."

Our rally court was the center of our high school. It was where everyone hung out. To mess with it was like a visiting football opponent disrespecting the home team's logo on the fifty-yard line. Completely uncool. And, apparently, Cupertino's cheerleading squad thought it would be cute to toilet-paper *our* rally court in *their* colors before school started. Completely uncool and unsmart.

It took only a few seconds for us to understand what our coach had just said. But once we did, all the wrestlers and water polo players flew out of the weight room in a full sprint through the empty halls toward the rally court.

So, let's push pause on this story for now. Little did I realize I was about to become a victim of mental jiujitsu.

Flip Someone's Brain with Mental Jiujitsu

The martial art of jiujitsu can allow a smaller, weaker person to successfully defend themselves against a bigger, stronger, heavier opponent by using leverage and weight distribution to obtain an advantageous position. In jiujitsu, as in wrestling, you often use your opponent's energy against them. You rarely match strength with strength.

Naturally, when you think of jiujitsu, you think of . . . Jesus, Gandhi, and Martin Luther King.

(I'll admit it. That sounds like a great setup for a joke: Jesus, Gandhi, and MLK walk into a bar . . .)

Irreverence aside, it was these three guys—among others— who preached what I call the art of mental jiujitsu. They called it turning the other cheek or going the extra mile (Jesus), conquering with love (Gandhi), and meeting the forces of hate with the power of love (MLK).

I'll let them speak for themselves; here's what they preached:

Jesus:

>Whosoever shall smite thee on thy right cheek, turn to
>him the other also. And if any man will sue thee at the

law, and take away thy coat, let him have thy cloak also. And whosoever shall compel thee to go a mile, go with him twain. (Matthew 5:39–41)

Gandhi:

Whenever you are confronted with an opponent, conquer him with love.

MLK:

Hate begets hate; violence begets violence; toughness begets a greater toughness. We must meet the forces of hate with the power of love.[79]

I'm not trying to turn this into a religious revival. If you've read my other books, you know I shy away from making my books about religion. When others start citing scripture to prove their point, I get kinda cynical. I can feel my willingness to learn start to shut down. Over the years, however, I've made a conscious effort to not be totally closed-minded when I hear things I disagree with, or that make me uncomfortable, or that challenge what I believe. In fact, that's the very thing I advocate for in this book as I encourage you to open your mind.

When I encounter these moments now, I try to pause, take a deep breath, and listen because I've found that wisdom and truth are often found at the most uncomfortable times and in the most uncomfortable situations. We need to humble ourselves a bit and open our hearts. With an open mind, we can find truth and inspiration—and even common ground. As my father would tell me, "Art, you need to listen with your heart *and* your head. They have to be on the same page."

So, what can Jesus, Gandhi, and MLK teach us about mental jiujitsu?

Quite a bit, actually.

But first, let me tell another story from high school and one of my first practices with using mental jiujitsu to escape a potential physical beatdown.

Picking a Fight with the Trans-Am Guy and His Friends

What is it with me and water balloons? Why hasn't anyone staged a water-balloon intervention with me by now?

First, there was the water-balloon incident with my youth leader, which resulted in his meltdown, and now this.

It was the summer of 1978, and we were going to be high school seniors.

My buddies and I were out cruising around town in two VW Beetles. The little bugs had moonroofs, and we had an ample supply of water balloons. Whenever we saw a target, we drove by and the gunners popped out of the moonroofs and launched our arsenal, after which we sputtered away, laughing. Of course, we hit nothing most of the time, but the intent and shock factor were all we needed.

As we cruised past the back of our high school, Monta Vista, we couldn't believe what we saw.

Parked near the back entrance and leaning up against a T-top Trans Am—just like in the movie *Smokey and the Bandit*—were three smarmy dudes wearing letterman jackets from one of our rival high schools, Lynbrook. And to top it off, there they were chatting up three girls from our school who were clearly enamored with this overcompensating car and who were flirting right back at them.

If ever there was a time the universe was crying out for a group of teenage boys to shock-and-awe some rival high school wannabes with a volley of water balloons, this was it.

I instructed the driver of our bug to approach slowly. I was gunner on this sortie and readying to launch. The other Beetle hung back to see what would happen.

You know how sharks kinda cruise up slow and then, in the blink of an eye, unleash their fury on their victims? That was how our little bug approached our target. The dude and his two buddies were distracted by the girls, and the girls were distracted by the flashy Trans Am. None of them noticed the slow little bug moving into position.

As we pulled even with the Trans Am, I popped out of the moonroof and fired.

And splash! It was a perfect shot.

The water balloon arced and wobbled through the air almost in slow motion, sailing right in front of the driver's face and landing on his center console, exploding water all over the leather interior of his prized Trans Am.

I was stunned by the accuracy of my throw and the damage to the inside of his newly detailed ride. There was water everywhere. The shock on their faces was priceless.

We, the ballooners, erupted in cheers and laughter.

But we didn't have much time to celebrate.

Because the chase was on.

Mr. Trans Am and friends were enraged. And they were in a car we couldn't outrun.

But we didn't care. They hadn't noticed the other VW Bug in our armada, carrying three other guys and following them following us.

So if Mr. Trans Am caught us, no biggie. We had two bugs with six guys total against one Trans Am with three. I'll take those odds any day.

After they trailed us for several miles, it was clear they weren't going to stop until they confronted us. I told our driver to pull into a cul-de-sac.

"What, are you crazy?" my buddies asked me. "We'll be trapped for sure."

"I'll take care of it."

"We're not getting out of the car with you," they said. They were definitely not confrontation-type people. Instead of in-your-face victims, they were the type who quietly seethed from a distance.

"I got it," I said with confidence. I mean, I was filled with bravado. Our other bug was right behind the Trans Am. And that bug held three guys who didn't mind hopping out and having my back in a tussle should the need arise. But I was utterly convinced it would not come to that.

Our vehicle pulled into a cul-de-sac and parked. The Trans Am screeched to a halt behind us. I was already out of our bug, striding assertively toward the Trans Am.

The driver was yelling, and I was defiantly chuckling. I couldn't wait to see the looks on their faces when the cavalry pulled up behind them and my other buddies hopped out brazenly, tilting the odds in our favor. The guys in the Trans Am wouldn't be talking so tough in about ten seconds.

"You're gonna clean my car, punk," he yelled.

"Who's gonna make me clean it? You?" I replied mockingly, as if I were the toughest guy in the world.

"Yeah, we'll make you clean it."

"Ooooh yeeeeaaaah?" I said sardonically.

"And then I'm ripping you to pieces," he threatened.

Bottom line, he and his friends were going to make me clean his car, or I'd be sorry.

I waited for my trap to be sprung so I could turn the tables on them. And that thought only amped up my boldness, arrogance, and smack-talking.

As I faced them, I could see the entrance of the cul-de-sac where it intersected with the main street. I could hear the approach of the other Beetle with its jangly little engine. It slowed on the main street as it approached the turn into the cul-de-sac.

I was a bit giddy.

These Trans Am guys are gonna eat some crow, I thought.

But my reinforcements and I had a miscommunication. They slowed. I waved, trying to signal to them that they were right on time and to come to the rescue.

But they thought I was waving them off because everything was cool and I didn't need them.

So off my reinforcements drove, leaving me to deal with the dangerous, volatile situation I had just created.

The sound of the VW Beetle driving past the cul-de-sac and down the road out of sight was more than a bit unsettling.

And the three angry jocks stalking toward me right then had no idea what had just happened.

Now I wasn't so giddy. Now I wasn't so brave.

Now I felt more than a quiver of worry.

I had to do something to put out the fuse I had lit and deescalate the situation. I needed some mental jiujitsu—and fast.

"You're gonna be cleaning my car without any teeth," he yelled.

I happened to like my teeth and was hoping not to lose them so soon in life, so I said to him, "Hey, do you have any towels? What do you have that I can use to clean up your car?"

I changed my tone of voice and even my demeanor and stance. The switch from Mr. Tough Guy to "Hey, let me wipe that up for you" was so fast and head-spinning it completely disarmed the Trans Am three-man gang. "Uh, I don't know. Let me check." Soon, with some improvised towels, I dried the dashboard and seats.

"Sorry about that," I said.

"Yeah, well, might want to think twice next time."

With all my teeth, I got back into our car and breathed a sigh of relief.

My encounter with Trans-Am guy was a great lesson for me in how to turn the tables. Although at the time, as a high school kid who was focused largely on self-preservation, my actions benefitted everyone involved. It was the right thing to do. When you use mental Jiujitsu to stop anger, aggression, and violence, it promotes love for all.

What's even better, however, and part and parcel with a Ruby Rule mentality, is when you can take that mental jiujitsu to the next level by doing the right thing *for the right reason*, which is what Christ, Gandhi, and King advocated.

Don't Flip the Bird; Flip the Power Structure

In my Trans-Am story, I had to quickly shift the aggressive and uncompromising think pattern of my brain. I had to quickly reprogram to a stance of humility, sincerity, and willingness to do something nice for someone who had every right to be angry at me and whom I had just been arrogantly taunting. I needed to practice mental jiujitsu to achieve a state of something I call civil restraint.

Yes, I was forced into the situation, so no bonus points for me. But the power of mental jiujitsu—a great tactic for establishing a Vault and finding common ground (two foundational tactics for becoming a shoe-shifting Ruby Rule practitioner)—was that it flipped the power structure regardless of my original intent or the new intent forced upon me.

This idea of flipping the power structure has been preached by Gandhi, MLK, and Christ, and it's intimately tied to my concept of mental jiujitsu.

The great gurus of peace—Gandhi, MLK, and Christ—conceived of it as something the two twentieth-century men called civil disobedience and Christ called turning the other cheek. I prefer to call it civil restraint.

The philosophy is, in my opinion, so misunderstood. Christ, Gandhi, and King were not suggesting we roll over and allow others to abuse us, to shut up and take it.

Not at all. We don't show love to others by letting them abuse us. They are, in actuality, not only hurting us; they are hurting themselves. Unless there's some severe psychosis illness going on, no one can truly feel good about themselves when demeaning or abusing others.

Civil disobedience, or civil restraint, is a way of protesting against injustice while recognizing that those who see things from a different perspective are fellow human beings worthy of our respect and love. It embodies humility, humanity, and hope in a nonviolent manner when one individual or group is trying to oppress others.

The civil disobedience taught and practiced by Christ (with the Pharisees and Sadducees, the ultimate hypocrites of their day), Gandhi (in his stand against British oppression), and King (who countered prejudice and enjoined unity between people regardless of race)—and others—has brought about amazing, positive change for billions on this earth. This positive change was not brought about by hate, fighting, or war but by humility, humanity, and hope.

One of the best ways to understand civil restraint is to try to understand what it is not. Civil restraint is not vengeful retaliation. It is not egotistical cruelty driven by despair and hopelessness. Civil restraint does not provoke, bully, or harass your oppressor.

Civil restraint is a calm, self-controlled, *compassionate* response in the face of hostility, oppression, and condescending arrogance. Civil restraint recognizes the oppressor or antagonist as a human being worthy of humanity. But it also recognizes that despite being human, the oppressor and antagonist is off the path of politeness and kindness. The oppressor has a sense of superiority about them as demonstrated by their words and actions. When you invoke civil restraint, you are responding with love, self-control, and a sense of inner security.

Civil restraint's main objective is to expose injustice while simultaneously deescalating the tension and explosiveness of the conflict. You want the oppressor to come to their own conclusion that their behavior is out of line and that their perceived superiority is the problem because if you try to force them to change their mind, it almost assuredly won't work. In fact, it may entrench them further in their belief that they are right.

So you must practice some mental jiujitsu, flipping the oppressor's perceived power against them.

This mental jiujitsu is based on the principle of civil restraint. We confront the oppressor without hostility, aggression, or threats because we recognize their worth as a human being.

Sometimes the oppressor is so lost in their self-importance they may not come to the conclusion we want. But guess what? When we pull some mental jiujitsu out of our Ruby Rule bag of tricks, others will likely be influenced by it—even if the oppressor with whom we are engaged doesn't.

Again, civil restraint is not being a human doormat, allowing anyone, anywhere to walk all over you. It is also not fight or flight. Civil restraint is about calmly and deliberately taking control of the situation and helping all involved to see and understand the injustice happening. It is about the creation and actualization of metanoia.

Nurturing Metanoia

What is metanoia? Is it contagious? Is there a cure?

Well, good news. Metanoia is a condition you want. And we're hoping it's very contagious. Fingers crossed it has no cure.

Metanoia means "a change of heart, remorse, and repentance." In the King James Version of the Bible, it is often translated as "to repent" or "repentance."[80]

Metanoia is the goal of mental jiujitsu and civil restraint.
We want:

1. To jiujitsu our brains when we feel wronged so we don't react
   in anger or harbor thoughts of hostility and revenge
2. After we flip our natural reaction, to practice civil restraint
   to inspire change by not fighting anger with anger or battling
   hate with hate

We aren't out to condemn or shame the antagonist. We want
to lead them to an epiphany that their actions are causing pain
and negative outcomes, not only for others but for themselves;
we want them to have a change of heart because we care about
the happiness of all involved, including the antagonist's.

I know. I suppose it sounds kinda hippy, peace-love-freedom
naïve. But if it does that sound way, then Jesus, Gandhi, and
King were the ultimate hippies.

Don't believe me? Let's pick apart three of Christ's parables that
teach the essence of turning the other cheek and peaceful protest,
the very heart of Gandhi's and King's methodologies as well.

Parable 1: "Hey, loser, carry my stuff—or else."

Here's what Jesus says in Matthew 5:41: "And whosoever shall
compel thee to go a mile, go with him twain."

So who the heck is compelling Jews in the first century to
walk a mile—and why?

It was Roman soldiers. Roman law at the time permitted a
Roman soldier to draft any Jewish citizen to carry his gear for
one mile.

If you were Jewish and had a ton of stuff to get done that
day, too bad. Not a big fan of abusive and arrogant Roman soldiers occupying your nation? Too bad. Back sore from a pulled

muscle you got digging a well? Too bad. If you refused the order to carry the soldier's gear for a mile, you could (and likely would) be publicly flogged and imprisoned.

So that sucks.

But on the bright side, the law limited the distance of this forced Sherpa-hood to one mile. Hit the mile mark and you could put the soldier's dirty, sweaty junk on the ground, turn around, and head back to what you were doing before being enlisted.

Jesus is asking his followers to do something remarkable. If you find yourself carrying a Roman soldier's equipment one mile down the hot, dusty road because you've been compelled to, Jesus says you should politely offer to carry the soldier's equipment another mile.

No strings attached.

No ulterior motive.

No passive-aggressive seething as you do it.

And this is a parable, so Jesus isn't just giving advice for one specific situation a Jew might find themselves in.

So, why? Why would Jesus ask something that seems so counterintuitive and difficult? This is the essence of how Jesus wants his disciples to live their lives: when dealing with your enemies, antagonists, and oppressors—those who have power over you and who wield that power in ways that are unpleasant for you—you should offer to do more for this antagonist.

Totally bizarre.

You lugged the load one mile because you had to. You were essentially a slave. But the second mile? Now you just turned the tables.

You mentally jiujitsued that centurion and flipped the script, so to speak. How? Because at the final step of one mile, you are entirely within your rights to drop his stuff and run back home.

But you don't.

Why? You now own the second mile. You are doing it of your own free will. You are acting as a free person. You show humility, humanity, and hope. You are demonstrating dignity, strength, and self-respect. What's more, you are humanizing that soldier. After all, he may be fighting a battle you know nothing about. Those who treat others with disdain do it because they are insecure or misguided in some way. Those who are truly at peace with who they are, like Christ, Gandhi, and King, treat others with kindness and dignity.

Just close your eyes and try to imagine this scene: For the first mile, the soldier, most likely bigger and stronger than you, is more than capable of carrying his own sweaty, stinky, grimy stuff. Gruffly, he interrupts you from whatever you're doing and demands you haul his stuff.

Can you see his smirk as he walks beside you? You are no better than a donkey to him. "Faster!" he barks at you every fifty yards.

You stumble under the weight a bit as he hurls insults in your direction. If he's in a particularly foul mood, he spits at you.

At last, you reach the end of the mile. He's probably scanning the area for the next Jew to conscript. But you speak up and calmly, kindly say, "Why don't I help you with the next mile as well?"

Think of how the Roman soldier might feel at that moment. He treated you like dirt—and even if he didn't, he forced you to do something you did not want to do. He probably expects hostility and scorn.

He does not expect this.

Of course, he may think you're trying to curry favor with the occupiers.

But what if your dignified and self-composed manner forces the soldier to see you as more than an inferior? And more than that, what if his humanity is touched? Might it cause him to be kinder to the next soul he conscripts to carry his things? Might he feel a twinge of regret? You've treated him as a person of worth, with consideration and perhaps even love.

This move toward a metanoia epiphany may not happen for the soldier; he could greedily accept your offer and keep yelling at you the whole second mile.

But regardless, you are not fighting oppression with hate. You are "fighting" it with love. And regardless of how effective your act is on the oppressor, what does going the second mile do to your sense of self, confidence, and character? You grow. You become a stronger person. Maybe you do this enough times that you encounter soldiers who have empathy. You share stories of your families and find things in common. Maybe it doesn't change the political landscape all at once, but it can definitely change the inner-soul landscape of oppressed and oppressor. And in a way, that's exactly what Christ wants from his disciples: care for the one, outreach to the individual.

And that's what I'm trying to articulate as I write about the Ruby Rule and its power to effect change.

In this way, civil restraint flips the script. The true beauty of it is that while we raise the victim's status, we also raise the antagonist's by humanizing him and treating him with kindness. It's a Ruby-style win-win.

Parable 2: "Give me your coat."

The second parable Jesus uses to teach this concept of civil restraint comes from Matthew 5:40: "And if any man will sue thee at the law, and take away thy coat, let him have thy cloak also."

Back in the first century, you typically wore an overcoat and an undercoat. These layers made it easy to add or remove garments depending on the temperature of the day.

So Jesus said that if, for any reason, someone sued you for your outercoat, you gave them your undercoat as well.

This is the same principle as going the extra mile. How? When you owe some neighbor a few bucks, and you're down on your luck, and the neighbor sues you and approaches you in the town square with a court order that mandates you to give him your "outercoat," Jesus wants you to say to that neighbor: "Oh, hi, Otis Ben-Issachar. Sorry about those shekels I owe you. But as long as you're taking my outercoat, please take the undercoat as well. It is of the finest quality and will serve you well. The two coats are a set, made from the finest camel skin and lined with imported silk. You're out in the weather quite a bit, and having both would really benefit you."

Remember how Sarah Silverman diffused hostility and anger with a kind, caring response? Here again, you've treated the antagonist in a way you hope encourages them to shift from a state of aggression, dominance, and oppression to a state of metanoia.

Will humility emerge? Maybe. Maybe not. But maybe the antagonist feels a tiny bit of your compassion. And their tone and actions now and in the future may be softened. We flip the power because we know how good it feels to be at peace and we care about the other person; we hope that in feeling the love, they will possibly have a change of heart and feel a bit of that inner peace as well.

What if there are others watching? This interaction would most likely be happening in the agora (public square), with many witnesses. Some might start to wonder what's going on. There's a chance some will turn on the bully and say, "Hey, this isn't fair. He has no right to do that. He can legally ask only for the outercoat. What's going on?"

I mean, I like to imagine the crowd backing the underdog and angrily confronting the antagonist as he stands there holding both your outer- and inner coats.

"You got it all wrong," he might say. "I didn't ask for this. He just gave me the undercoat without me asking for it."

"Oh, *riiiiiight*," the crowd might say. "You've been suing people for their coats all over this town. You're a greedy coat hoarder!"

Nobody likes facing an angry mob. And now the antagonist is a bit nervous. The power has flipped and you are no longer the victim. Your actions have brought you a sense of peace, knowing the antagonist doesn't have the power to make you feel angry, resentful, or vengeful. You get to choose how to feel and how to act. You get to choose civil restraint as you strive to make a difference for your antagonist and for anyone who might be watching.

This may not happen at all. There may not be any witnesses. And maybe the bully doesn't change and keeps coming back to sue you for other things.

Even if that's what happens this time, your action subtly takes some of the power away from your enemy.

Parable 3: "It's happy-slappy time."

In Matthew 5:39, we find the parable about cheek-slappin': "But I say to you, Do not resist an evil-doer. But if anyone strikes you on the right cheek, turn the other also."

For whatever reason, we often shorten this quote to the cliché, "Turn the other cheek." It's easy to misinterpret this as justification for being passive and consenting to whatever injustice we observe or suffer. It's kind of like saying to yourself, "I will merely sit and do nothing in the hope that whatever or whoever is doing the bullying, abusing, molesting, or striking will just stop."

I always thought this parable was about hitting—the way two people would hit each other if they were in a fistfight. If my enemy throws a punch and hits me on my right cheek,

I shouldn't counter-punch. Instead, I should turn and let him throw another punch and hit me on my left cheek.

Maybe I think of it this way because of a fight I got into with Shawn Murphy in sixth grade.

Shawn and I were good buddies. But at recess one day, we got into an argument. The gist of our disagreement was determining which of us was the *real* king of the monkey bars.

We each claimed the title and refused to concede anything to the other. Smack-talking escalated to name-calling, then to yelling. Finally, Shawn uttered those words that were the sixth-grade vernacular for "I challenge you to a duel": "I'm calling you out, Coombs."

I didn't really want to fight, but now, with everyone watching, the pressure was on. "You got it," I said. "Name the time and place."

"Right after school at the back gate," he said.

This was where many schoolyard scuffles took place. It was just off school grounds and out of sight of most of the teachers.

We got out of school at 3:00 p.m. By the time I made it to the back gate, a large crowd had gathered. In the center of the circled crowd was Shawn waiting for me.

I was twelve, and this would be my first real schoolyard skirmish. I entered the circle and faced Shawn. We stared at each other. The crowd started chanting, "Fight! Fight! Fight!"

Then, when we didn't immediately charge each other in bloodlust, someone behind me pushed me and I lunged toward Shawn.

He didn't see that I had been pushed. He just saw me suddenly moving aggressively toward him. It's true I was aggressively trying to keep my balance so I didn't face-plant at the feet of my opponent and look stupid.

Shawn's fists flailed at me, and the fight was on.

Well, sorta; this fight could scarcely be called a fight. It was kind of like a slow-motion collision of thrashing limbs. If smartphones had existed, my "fight" would have gone viral as a comedic clip labeled "PUNCH FAIL!"

But now it only exists as an embarrassing memory of my childhood. And, by the way, it stands as a sterling example of exactly what Jesus was telling us NOT to do. A lesson that would take me years to learn.

After studying this turn-the-other-cheek parable in-depth, I've concluded that this is one of the most misunderstood verses in the Bible.

Civil restraint is about truth and justice. It is not about apathetically sitting back and allowing liars and perpetrators to walk all over us. It's about acting in a way that can prompt metanoia in the offender's heart and head so they come to their own conclusion that their behavior is uncivil and inappropriate.

Let's start with the statement, "Do not resist an evildoer."

Here, Christ is saying we should never retaliate against hostility with hostility, never respond violently to those who are evil.

Notice that Jesus is not saying we should do nothing. I believe he's defining "resist" as "struggle against;" in other words, don't fight hate in kind.

Okay. Difficult to achieve, but definitely something to aspire to. But the parable doesn't end there.

Next, it says, "If anyone strikes you on the right cheek, turn the other also."

This is where it gets interesting. Why does Jesus call out the right cheek? This is a parable, so every detail is significant in conveying the symbolic meaning.

Back in Jesus's time, the left hand was considered unclean. The first century was a right-handed century. In most cultures, especially those in and around the Red Sea and the Mediterranean, the left hand was used only for unclean activities. For example, you wiped yourself with your left hand. That was common knowledge. There was no toilet paper, and the left hand was reserved for the uglier things in life. It does not get much uglier than wiping yourself. That falls in the disgustingly gross, unclean category.

So we can be sure the offender doing the smiting would have been using their right hand. Because even if you're slapping or striking an underling, you'd still not use your left hand ... unless you were delivering the ultimate, degrading insult. Maybe if you had captured an enemy in battle or caught the murderer of someone you loved.

Now, if the offender was using their right hand and smiting a subordinate's right cheek, there was only one way to make that happen, and that was a backhanded slap. This denoted a reprimand or insult, not an all-out fistfight, and was the customary way to admonish someone over whom you had power.

So, now, with this background, let's try to picture this scene in our minds. Take the position of the oppressor. Let's envision you are the master of the house. You are wealthy, powerful, and have prominent status in the community.

You're walking to the public square one day to buy some goods. Your servant reluctantly tags along to help you carry the groceries and parcels back to the house. But the whole time you're walking to the public square, the servant isn't performing up to your exacting standards. You think he looks a bit unkempt, he isn't moving fast enough, and he doesn't bow deep enough in showing respect to you and other superiors you encounter while he grumbles under his breath.

Maybe he carelessly drops items you've given him to carry, embarrassing you in front of your peers. Finally, you've had enough, and you give your servant a light backhanded, right-handed slap across his right cheek.

You would expect the response you have always gotten when in similar situations. In fact, if someone superior to you gave you a backhand, you would respond the same way the master expected the slave to respond. You would cower a bit while submitting meekly. But this time your slave calmly and confidently turns and offers you his left cheek, even as the right cheek reddens from the first blow.

Your servant isn't cowering or apologizing. What do you do now?

Well, you're the master of the house. You set the standards and enforce them. And now your slave is being a bit cheeky—pun intended. You've got to teach him another lesson, right? If he wants another slap, you can oblige. Maybe the servant will then quietly submit and get on with serving you up to the expected level of service and precision.

You want to strike him, but with his right cheek turned away from you and his left cheek offered as a wide-open target, you'd need to strike him with your left hand because you don't want to slap him with your palm and indicate he is a higher status than a slave. So you would need to deliver a left-handed backhand. And that would force you to commit an unclean act with your unclean left hand.

In that culture and time, you would never write, wave to someone, touch another with, or eat with your left hand. Yeah, would you want to eat with the same hand you use to wipe? The thought alone gives this germaphobe literal cold chills.

You pause. *I can't slap him with my left hand*, you think. It would be a massive social *faux pas*—even from master to servant.

How about striking him with your right hand again? Problem solved.

Not quite. You can't backhand him again . . . not unless you want to connect with his skull and hurt your hand. Then you'll look particularly foolish in the public square. A master howling in pain, hopping up and down and holding your bruised and maybe broken hand—humiliated by a servant! You won't hear the end of it.

You could slap him with an open right palm. But that would mean you're striking him as an equal. According to the custom at that time, in a fight, equals slapped each other open-handed or with closed fists.

The entire day has been a bit frustrating, and now you are utterly confused. You still haven't gotten what you came for, and now this dust-up with your servant. Ugh. What to do? Exasperated, you could have your servant flogged, but do you really want to go that far? Hasn't your servant already made his point? If you have him flogged publicly with twenty lashes, he will most likely turn and ask for twenty more—using your left hand? Where does it end?

Through civil restraint, your servant has made a stand—a nonviolent, restrained form of resistance. His message to you and all watching is that he's a human being who deserves your humanity, even though you hold immense power over them.

So what is Jesus teaching? He's not telling us to roll over and meekly accept injustice. No, he is challenging us to oppose evil, incivility, and persecution without resorting to anger or violence.

Jesus's parable invites us to use civil restraint in a way that hopefully forces an antagonist to be mindful of you and be confronted with the realization that they are not treating another human being with the worth, dignity, and humanity that human being deserves.

Sometimes, many times perhaps, this result won't happen.

But Jesus is clear. He wants us to always turn the other cheek. We can do this by constantly looking for creative ways to challenge effectively, actively, and nonviolently those who want to exploit and oppress in major or minor ways.

Your civil restraint can help the antagonist move toward a state of metanoia, all without using incivility, violence, anger, or hatred—just as Christ, Gandhi, and King advocated. To do this shows true strength and civility—and is the ultimate mental jiujitsu.

I Don't Disagree

In a business negotiation, I learned that one manifestation of mental jiujitsu is verbal jiujitsu. This is a simple, diplomatic—and civil—way to steer a conversation away from negative energy and potential confrontation. You might try it as you engage in conversation with those you disagree with.

I was in a conference room, heavy in negotiations for a major deal. At times, when I was questioning details of the deal and challenging specific points, the woman I was negotiating with would answer my sometimes-assertive queries by calmly saying, "I don't disagree."

Rationally, that meant, "I agree."

At some point deep in the meeting, she said it again as we navigated around a potential sticking point.

I paused and asked her, "When you say 'I don't disagree,' does that mean you agree?"

With a hint of a smile, she said, "No, not exactly."

"So what do you mean all these times you've been telling me 'I don't disagree'?"

She said, "I say it to avoid stalling the discussion."

Wow, what honesty. She was telling me that the result was more important than the minutiae. She was coyly deflecting her differing opinion on some minor details so my ego didn't obstruct a win-win.

As I reflect, "I don't disagree" is a clever way to keep the dialogue moving until both parties are happy. Saying "I disagree" could entrench both sides or stop negotiations altogether. It opens the door to negative, hackles-raising energy. And once that starts, it quickly escalates into incivility.

When negotiating or merely chatting about emotional issues, it may be wise to say, "I don't disagree" (even if you disagree with the other person) to avoid a stalemate or escalation.

In my case, we closed the deal, and both parties were happy with the results. I was grateful for my counterpart's rhetorical dexterity.

While I think we should say what we mean and mean what we say, I have learned that sometimes wily diplomacy is far more effective than brutal candor.

And yes, I can hear you saying, "I don't disagree."

Smart-aleck.

Showdown at the Rally Court; Or How I Was Jiujitsued into Metanoia

And now, back to the story about those rival cheerleaders toilet-papering our high school. If you'll remember, we left off in 1976, and we, the wrestlers and water polo athletes of Monta Vista High, had just been informed by our coach that some of the cheerleaders from the rival Cupertino High were toilet-papering our rally court on the day of the big game. And all of us adrenaline- and testosterone-fueled dudes had just run out to stop this atrocity.

Sure enough, there they were—about ten cheerleaders from Cupertino High.

They looked pretty cute in their maroon-and-gold cheer uniforms. But that didn't distract us (too much) from the crime they were committing: hurling maroon-and-gold toilet paper all over our school property.

Within a few frantic minutes, the cheerleaders were rounded up and detained. There was no way they could escape two dozen wrestlers and about fifteen water-polo players.

We brought our prisoners of war to the middle of the rally court and had them sit on a picnic table. Then we sorta stared at each other. What now?

One wrestler said we should watch them as they cleaned it all up and then let them go.

Reasonable.

But not as appealing (at least to the majority at that time) as the idea pitched by one of the water-polo players: "Let's tie the head cheerleader to the picnic table. We let the others go, but we don't release the head cheerleader until Cupertino's football team comes and negotiates the freedom of the hostage."

We (more like the senior leaders of the group) quickly voted on the second option. The motion was carried, the plan enacted, and we tied the head cheerleader to a bench on one side of the picnic table. We even used much of the toilet paper the cheerleaders had brought, and we wrapped her like a mummy.

Satisfied with our hostage situation, we told the others to go. Some of the Cupertino cheerleaders did not want to leave their leader there. They whined and pleaded with us but to no avail. To prove we were not heartless, we put a pillow under the prisoner's head and promised that no harm would come to her. But our terms remained. She would be released when the football team returned to get her.

We felt victorious as we watched the rest of the cheerleaders leave the campus, knowing they would have to deliver the news to their football team. We also knew it was about fifteen minutes from our school to theirs by car. So we had about forty-five minutes to an hour to wait for the football team to show.

That young lady remained mummified in our rally court all that time.

Nearly a full hour, man.

She never cried, and she didn't seem overtly angry. Was she irked? Yes, at first, but then she felt more and more at ease. While we all took our promise to protect her seriously, a few athletes saw it as a great opportunity for conversation. Over the next half hour, some of the water-polo players began flirting with her, and a few even earnestly asked her out.

In this situation, we had turned into the antagonists who now held the power to oppress and dehumanize another group. When I think about that situation now, I am supremely embarrassed. Had I been that young lady's father, I would have been beyond upset. Their dishonor to our school did not warrant this response.

Still, it blows me away how different times are these days. Not only did we tie her up while the entire school looked on (teachers included) as they began arriving for school, but we took a picture that made it into the yearbook. With a few water-polo players smiling behind the picnic table, she lay horizontal and immobile like she was some wild game we had just caught and we were proud hunters.

Try to imagine that. A young lady was tied to a bench in the middle of our high school rally court while more than two thousand kids looked on. How many teachers walked by and did nothing? Just kids being kids? Makes me shudder to this day.

We were wrong to tie her up, even if it was meant to be in fun—just like my nuclear water balloon on Doug Miller's back was meant to be fun. Given the opportunity, I would apologize to that young lady.

As our other classmates got to school, I remember that many members of our football team had congregated with us and were happy about our plan.

There must have been more than one hundred high school athletes waiting there, getting more and more amped up as they anticipated a potentially hostile confrontation with a group of rival athletes.

So what would our rival high school football team do? Would they come in acting tough, determined to save their honor? Would a few show up or their entire school? Would it be an all-out brawl, or would we choose our individual champions and send them to settle it in one-on-one gladiatorial combat? We knew the rival guys would be mad as hell, so we braced ourselves for hostility, ready for anything.

Sure enough, just before 8:00 a.m., someone down the walk called out, "They're coming!"

It was just like an old Western where the hapless extra shouts out the arrival of the bad guys, or good guys—who really knows? Instantly, all our emotions and tension ratcheted up. Other kids who were on the lookout sprinted into the court, screaming, "They're here! They're here!" Our athletes gathered in a semi-circle behind the hostage, who was now untied and patiently waiting to be liberated.

But when the Cupertino High Pioneers football team rounded the corner into the rally court and we saw what they wore, we were confused. Every single one of them had on his lettermen's jacket; we were expecting that.

What we weren't expecting were the cheap, white cowboy hats they all had on. They looked small on some of the guys, which made them look even sillier. These large, tough football players looked ridiculous and entirely out of character—while at the same time looking strangely cool.

Slowly, everything made sense. Their mascot was a cowboy-hat-wearing pioneer, and those cowboy hats were part of the band's uniform. That explained how they got so many hats so quickly. The ridiculousness of it made us all crack a smile. Even the cheerleader who was in the center of it all let out a snicker and shook her head in disbelief. All our intense emotions melted immediately, the anxiety and anticipation of a confrontation gone.

We had been mentally jiujitsued on a grand scale. The Cupertino High Pioneers football team knew they had to come and represent their school, but they also knew they did not want trouble.

The cowboy hats were symbolic of many things. They were good-guy white. White also represented peace and surrender. And in a way, that's what they were doing (while maintaining their dignity).

They were calm as can be, humble, witty, and self-deprecating. Oddly, it made them all that much cooler, all that much stronger. A few even grinned as we made the hostage exchange. As we chatted with some of them, they laughed, and we laughed with them. They were not the enemy. They were not different from us. They were just like us.

Toward the end, a few football players jokingly commented that if their cheerleaders ever did something stupid like that again, all we had to do was give them a call and they would come take care of it.

At this, the now-free head cheerleader cheekily called out, "Hey, whose side are you on?" The players' appearance, attitudes, and playful teasing back and forth deescalated what could have been a rough morning for all involved.

Because our rival team practiced civil restraint, it made the soil of our hearts fertile for the seeds of metanoia to take root and change us. They flipped the script, and we were all better for it.

Again, I would love to find that cheerleader and express regret on behalf of one young, stupid, sophomore wrestler who was not strong enough to put a stop to the prisoner plan when it started.

Thankfully, what could have been a very ugly situation turned enemies into friends.

And that is the essence of the Ruby Rule I'm advocating for in this book: to approach situations with those we view as enemies and hostiles with civil restraint, ready to practice mental jiujitsu and inspire metanoia in those with whom we do not agree.

I mean, those with whom we don't disagree.

Chapter Recap

- Often, wisdom and truth are found at the most uncomfortable times and in the most uncomfortable situations.

- Civil restraint is a calm, self-controlled, compassionate response in the face of hostility, oppression, and condescending arrogance.

- When you invoke civil restraint, you respond with love, self-control, and inner security.

- Civil restraint is not being a human doormat, allowing anyone, anywhere to walk all over you. It is also not fight or flight. Civil restraint is about calmly and willfully taking control of the situation and helping all involved see and understand the injustice happening.

- *Metanoia* means "a change of heart, remorse, and repentance" and is the goal of mental jiujitsu and civil restraint. We want to inspire change—not fight anger with anger or battle hate with hate.

- "Whosoever shall smite thee on thy right cheek, turn to him the other also. And if any man will sue thee at the law, and take away thy coat, let him have thy cloak also. And whosoever shall compel thee to go a mile, go with him twain."

- If you are thinking about toilet-papering your rival high school the morning of the big game, don't!

Pause and Think

- Have you ever felt like someone was picking on you? Have you ever been bullied? Think about civil restraint and how this concept may help you the next time you get into a similar situation. What will you do differently? How can you practice some mental jiujitsu?

- Have you ever been the oppressor? Do the concepts discussed in this chapter prick your conscience and give you pause when it comes to how you treat others?

- How much humility do you exhibit while under pressure?

- If you find yourself in a conversation this week with someone with whom you disagree, try saying "I don't disagree" whenever they bring up a point you want to challenge. Write or talk about how that goes.

CONCLUSION

⬙

WHERE WE'VE BEEN, WHERE WE'RE GOING

I t is now time to wrap things up and ask, *Where do we go from here?*

Good question. I've made the case for each person reading this book to practice the Ruby Rule and civility—just as I've pledged to do.

And though our numbers may be few right now, I'm certain some of us will impact friends and family members not only by sharing some of the ideas contained in these pages but also by our Ruby-calibrated actions and efforts to act civilly and with love for all, even those with whom we adamantly disagree. The examples we set may inspire others, and if we can start a civility movement, just with ourselves and our own efforts, I am confident that movement will grow. Because goodness, kindness, friendliness, civility, and courtesy are contagious.

In fact, here's just one recent study that shows the contagious effect of simply being polite. Researchers at New York University found that "polite, unofficial warnings can reduce hate speech on Twitter."[81] In the study, researchers identified Twitter users who broadcasted high volumes of hate speech. They contacted these users not as an official warning from Twitter but as fellow Twitter users politely asking them to stop and providing a friendly reminder that they might draw attention from Twitter and get suspended. "Users who received polite suspension warnings from unofficial handles reduced hate speech by 15–20%."[82]

While the effect on the spewers of hate speech wasn't permanent (it lasted about thirty days), it shows the power of people engaging with each other in a constructive, civil way rather than screaming at and berating each other.

Now, for a quick recap. Just as I've ended each chapter with a recap, I will end the book with one.

The Heaviness of Hate

Let me end with how I began by asking:

Are you tired?

Are you like me and you're asking yourself how we got here? What have we become?

We have a serious problem. There's simply too much hatred in our world, our country, and in the hearts of too many. It would be hard to find a corner of the world that has true serenity. This is not a situation we should accept as okay, nor can humanity continue this way much longer.

Hate hangs in the air like jungle humidity, so thick and heavy you can cut it with a knife—and then eat it with a fork. I fear far too many find the hatred delicious.

We must work to rid our culture of contempt before it is all we know, need, and crave. Hate, once consumed, can only feed our appetite for more hate—and once we've digested the poison of hate, violence, destruction, and death will absolutely follow.

Mobs terrorize families in theaters, restaurants, and even in their own homes just because they have different political opinions. We have individuals mailing anthrax and pipe bombs to those they dislike. Innocent lives are being lost.

We have racism. Classism. Discrimination. Verbal and even physical fights—and the videos go viral.

Hateful online trolls attack strangers in the vilest of ways, stirring up a frenzy of distrust, misunderstanding, and disdain for those who are different in any way—to the delight of the instigators.

We have mass murders in synagogues, mosques, Sikh temples, Christian chapels, schools, grocery stores, shopping centers, concerts, clubs, and places of employment. Hatred and divisive opinions are spewed on news outlets and social media—all because someone has a different faith, pigment, gender, or point of view.

Why can't we share our opinions without offensive name-calling and worse?

Shameful politicians on ALL sides fail us when they've demonize, bully, and encourage their supporters to vilify and intimidate those who disagree with them.

We need to spread love as quickly as the hate that's being propagated. Because even though hate is a powerful force, love is more powerful. Hate destroys; love builds, creates, heals, unites, and inspires. But it also takes more time to cultivate.

When Bad News Spews, Gratitude Soothes

Major media outlets fail us when they don't present the facts simply and objectively. True, every person and organization operates on some inherent level of preconceived notions, preferences, and beliefs. But most journalists once sought to find the facts and report them accurately. Now, those types of journalists and news organizations are in the minority. It seems every "news report" today more closely resembles the editorial opinions of the past.

In addition to the fact that the news has an agenda (yes, even the news sources you like best and feel represent your beliefs have an agenda), the news also tends to focus our attention on the bad, depressing, and anxiety-inducing stories.

Being inundated with negative, pessimistic, biased stories harms our psyches. We find ourselves viewing reality with tainted, smudged glasses.

Fact: What you repeatedly think about grows. What you fill your mind with colors how you see and interpret your reality. We attract what we devote our thoughts, time, and attention to. If you want "it" to grow, dwell on *it*, talk about *it*, and you will attract *it*.

If you give hate, incivility, anger, and negativity your rapt attention, they will grow within you, become part of you, and you will attract like minds and events.

The most valuable freedom you have is to choose your thoughts. Choose them carefully.

Make sure that what you most ardently desire and hope for is positive, civil, inspiring, and uplifting. Because what you focus on grows. Ponder the good you want to be and want to see in others, and don't yearn for everyone to believe the same way you do. Yearn for everyone to respect each other's beliefs and to disagree in a civil, constructive way.

Do this because when you consistently ponder on what you ardently desire and manifest, it begins to shape you and the places in the world you touch and influence.

Be mindful of your emotions when watching or reading the news. If you start feeling anxious, irritated, or critical toward others, tell yourself that if you choose to dwell on negative thoughts and feelings, you'll attract more negativity. Those around you will feel and feed off your negative energy.

Fortunately, you get to choose what to focus on. This doesn't mean you never feel any negative thoughts or emotions. And it doesn't mean you should feel bad if you do. Everybody does. It's part of the human experience.

But choose to divert your focus from the negative and make a conscious effort to simply observe your thoughts and feelings rather than grab ahold of the negative and spiral downward. Being a detached observer of yourself can allow you to deescalate from the volatile. Then you can choose to turn your attention to something uplifting and positive.

When all else fails, start making a list in your head, on your phone, or in a notebook, of what you're grateful for. Challenge yourself to come up with a list of ten things. Then, when you get to ten, challenge yourself to come up with ten more.

Gratitude will always lift your spirits and make you feel better—no matter what the news reports.

Differences Are Not Only Good, They're Essential

I recognize we are a nation of differing opinions. Some believe in more government; others believe in less. Some believe in a more robust military. Others don't. Some want to assess more taxes on businesses; others want big tax breaks for businesses. Some believe we should eliminate all fossil fuels yesterday; others want a measured, softer approach. Some want to put up walls with restrictions; others want no border walls with fewer restrictions.

There are a thousand more opinions on a thousand more issues—issues that span from the global to the national to the regional to the state to the county to the city to the subdivision to the household. These are all opinions, opinions that ebb and flow, opinions that can be adjusted and compromised. But only if we are all willing to give and take. But when you demonize and hate the other side, compromise and progress die on the vine.

We must learn to embrace the opinions of others. Differing opinions are a good thing—the healthiest of things, in fact, for a vibrant culture of caring. However, opinions are not what this book is about. It is about hate and love, positive and negative energy, and humanity moving forward or regressing to the Dark Ages.

There is such a thing as free speech in America. I get that. No, I love that! It's our right as Americans. But to hate people, to tell others they don't deserve to have rights, and to actively try to intimidate people to get our way—I can't wrap my head around it. That is not an opinion. That is not free speech. That is hatred. It must stop.

By working together regardless of ideology, we can turn away from the dangerous precipice of division and find safety on common ground.

It begins with each of us showing consideration for others. It begins when we respect our laws and stop allowing and encouraging political discourse to devolve into mixed-martial arts. It begins when we strive to make our conversations a vault—a place where tolerance, respect, and trust for each are paramount. It begins when we stop talking and start listening.

There will always be someone with an opposing view. Just remind yourself to take a deep breath, count to ten, and do some shoe-shifting to see things from that opposing view. That person who holds that view is not your enemy. Our great common denominator is that we are human. That, in and of itself, should warrant decorum in our interactions with each other. Strive to increase the level of civility, respect, and even love.

It Ain't Easy to Love Your Enemy

You can love someone close and dear to you easily enough. But loving those who hate you? Loving your enemies? That is one of the most difficult tasks for humans to achieve. It takes a healthy dose of metanoia, or change of heart, to make it happen.

People aren't always going to get along. We aren't always going to love everyone around us. But we can stop the hate, the disrespect, the bigotry. We have the option to make a difference toward turning the dark tide simply by being nice to each other. And by trying to love, not hate, our enemies.

No matter how justified it might feel, however stimulating it might be in the heat of the moment, hate degrades and ultimately destroys everyone it touches.

To embrace love and ditch hate doesn't mean we concede our core values. It does require us to simply remember our rivals' humanity. No matter our wealth, race, age, faith, or gender, we are all ordinary people sharing this planet. And with that humble understanding, we must speak and interact with each other in a manner that tells others we respect who they are, what they believe, and that we are willing to listen to what they have to say without dismissing it out of hand because we already "know" we have the truth.

It's Time for Decency

In some situations, I do believe silence is violence. That's why it's critical that we avoid the pitfalls of self-censoring. Honest disagreement is healthy. We can learn from it, grow because of it, and compromise to address it.

Unfortunately, us versus them, black versus white, right versus left mindsets have left us in a gridlock that can be seen globally, nationally, and in our neighborhoods and even families. We need a little more grace, a little more Ruby Rule, and a little more civil restraint. We need a lot less instant certainty and a lot more metanoia.

To be clear, if I haven't elucidated this point already, feeling angry is okay. Anger is utterly acceptable; it can even be honorably moral in the face of oppressive injustice. But anger is not the problem. The problem is not dealing with the anger constructively and instead letting it fester and boil over into hate and hate-motivated actions.

Learning to love your enemy and practicing the Ruby Rule and civil restraint will prevent anger from growing into hate. We, as a society, as humanity, must not go there. Once hate is the norm, death, destruction, and misery wait in the wings.

Our right to life, liberty, and the pursuit of happiness is being threatened by the extreme fringes on both sides who claim to be protecting those rights. But, really, they're defending those things only for those who believe as they do.

Love, respect, honor, and civility. That's what we owe *everyone.* That's the only way I know to arrest the growth of anger, hate, and distrust poisoning the nation. It's the only way I know to put an end to its dreadful consequences.

The Great Divide

If you listen closely, you will hear the fanatical fringes of the political spectrum screaming the loudest that if you disagree with them, you are not worth listening to and your views are not only wrong but corrosive to society. In fact, if you *do* disagree in any kind of public way, you could be canceled.

We must not participate in the bullying and shaming of the fringes. We can talk, listen, and refuse to engage in oppressive tactics. Nor should we be cowed by the fringes.

There will be those who claim that if you love them, you must see the world as they do.

They are wrong.

Compassion and unconditional love are indifferent to your opinions. Real love does not give a rat's ass about your pious judgment or arrogant narrow-mindedness.

This book is my attempt to push back on those who want to pull us apart.

And that's it. This book is the fruit of thoughts that have been swirling in my mind for at least two or three years, maybe more.

So let's all say to hell with hate. Let's embrace the Ruby Rule and make this planet a place of peace. How? Let's level up our humanity from Gold to Platinum and Platinum to Ruby by:

1. Embracing productive not destructive arguments
2. Changing our perspective
3. Avoiding instant certainty
4. Resisting the cancel-culture movement
5. Opposing the eye-for-an-eye mindset
6. Learning to love our enemies
7. Recognizing and embracing light and truth
8. Speaking up instead of being silent
9. Creating vaulted conversations
10. Using civil restraint to bring about metanoia

Look around. You will quickly realize that now, more than ever, we need to do more than believe in civility and love. We need to ACT with civility and love. I truly believe that if we start doing this—even if it's just one of us who decides to start adhering more closely to the ideals of the Ruby Rule—it will lead to a civility movement. I think most in this country are hungry for it and ready to forge a new path. Ultimately, this can lead to more *us* and less *them,* more *listening* and less *labeling,* and more *healing* and less *hating.*

Because now is the time to act. Now is the time to love.

Now is the time to go Ruby.

NOTES

1. Brian Morton, "Falser Words Were Never Spoken," *New York Times,* August 29, 2011, https://www.nytimes.com/2011/08/30/opinion/falser-words-were-never-spoken.html.

2. Casey-Gane McCallah, "Rush Limbaugh's Most Racist Quotes: A Timeline of Destructive Commentary," *NewsOne,* February 17, 2021, https://newsone.com/16051/top-10-racist-limbaugh-quotes/.

3. Maleki, @mean_leftist, Twitter, https://twitter.com/mean_leftist/with_replies.

4. Adam Forgie, "Alex Jones, in Detail, Describes Killing, Eating Neighbors to Feed His Kids, May 1, 2020, https://kutv.com/news/nation-world/video-alex-jones-in-detail-describes-killing-neighbors-to-feed-to-his-kids.

5. Teaching Values.com, "The Universality of the Golden Rule in the World Religions," June 3, 2022, https://www.teachingvalues.com/goldenrule.html.

6. Adam Forgie, "Utah Had Highest Growth Rate in the Nation over Past Decade, Census Bureau Estimates," KUTV News, December 29, 2020, https://kutv.com/news/local/utah-had-highest-growth-rate-in-the-nation-over-past-decade-census-bureau-estimates.

7. *Utah Governor Candidates Release Ads Together Calling for Civility,* The Hill, YouTube, https://www.youtube.com/watch?v=TAbqiRFjox4.

8. Weber Shandwick in partnership with Powell Tate and KRC Research, *Civility in America 2019: Solutions for Tomorrow,* 2019, https://www.webershandwick.com/news/civility-in-america-2019-solutions-for-tomorrow/.

9. Ibid.

10. Art Coombs, *Don't Just Manage—Lead!* (Salt Lake City, UT: Scrivener, 2015), 35.

11. Boyd Matheson, "Instant Certainty Is the Enemy of Truth and Trust," *Deseret News*, January 10, 2019, https://www.deseret.com/2019/1/10/20662989/boyd-matheson-instant-certainty-is-the-enemy-of-truth-and-trust.

12. Ibid.

13. Keith Griffith, "REVEALED: Citizen 'Vigilante' App CEO Raged 'Find This F**K. . . . Close in on Him' after Identifying the Wrong Homeless Man as Wildfire Arsonist and Putting $30,000 Bounty on His Head," DailyMail, May 28, 2021, https://www.dailymail.co.uk/news/article-9629695/Citizen-CEO-demanded-f-company-launched-frenzied-manhunt-wrong-man.html.

14. Ibid.

15. Ibid.

16. Ibid.

17. Ibid.

18. "Parents Pack into Utah County Meeting to Protest Student Mask Mandate," NBC News NOW, YouTube, July 16, 2020, https://www.youtube.com/watch?v=jSX6ATwcWl8.

19. Ibid.

20. Ibid.

21. Boyd Matheson, "Instant Certainty Is the Enemy of Truth and Trust," *Deseret News*, January 10, 2019, https://www.deseret.com/2019/1/10/20662989/boyd-matheson-instant-certainty-is-the-enemy-of-truth-and-trust.

22. Emily A. Vogels, Monica Anderson, Margaret Porteus, Chris Baronavski, Sara Atske, Colleen McClain, Brooke Auxier, Andrew Perrin, and Meera Ramshankar, "Americans and 'Cancel Culture': Where Some See Calls for Accountability, Others See Censorship, Punishment," Pew Research Center, May 19, 2021, https://www.pewresearch.org/internet/2021/05/19/americans-and-cancel-culture-where-some-see-calls-for-accountability-others-see-censorship-punishment/.

23. Ibid.

24. Clyde McGrady, "The Strange Journey of 'Cancel,' from a Black-Culture Punchline to a White-Grievance Watchword," *Washington Post*, April 2, 2021, https://www.washingtonpost.com/lifestyle/cancel-culture-background-black-culture-white-grievance/2021/04/01/2e42e4fe-8b24-11eb-aff6-4f720ca2d479_story.html.

25. Val Razo, "Understand the Versatility and Necessity of Hashtag Activism," Learn Hub, September 1, 2020, https://learn.g2.com/hashtag-activism.

26. Ligaya Mishan, "The Long and Tortured History of Cancel Culture," *New York Times*, December 3, 2020.

27. Jennifer Graham, "Chris Pratt Isn't Joining His Fellow Avengers in a Fundraiser for Joe Biden, and Twitter Piled On," *Deseret News*, December 19, 2020.

28. Ryan Parker and Aaron Couch, "'The Mandalorian' Star Gina Carano Fired Amid Social Media Controversy," *Hollywood Reporter*, February 10, 2021.

29. Ibid.

30. Ibid.

31. Ibid.

32. Marcos Martínez, "Burned to Death Because of a Rumour on Whatsapp," BBC News, November 12, 2018, https://www.bbc.com/news/world-latin-america-46145986.

33. Eli Meixler, "Five Killed in Latest Mob Attack After Rumors on Social Media: Here's What to Know About India's WhatsApp Murders," *Time*, July 3, 2018.

34. Joe Villasana, "Police: Texas Man Believed Social Media Rumors About Brother's Killer, Killed Innocent Man: Police Urge Texans to Use 'Caution and Common Sense' on Social Media," KWTX News, April 30, 2021.

35. Bari Weiss, "Resignation Letter," BariWeiss.com, https://www.bariweiss.com/resignation-letter.

36. Bari Weiss, "The Self-Silencing Majority: In Red America and Blue America, an Epidemic of Self-Censorship Is Threatening Democracy," *Deseret News*, March 2, 2021.

37. Bari Weiss, "Resignation Letter," BariWeiss.com, https://www.bariweiss.com/resignation-letter.

38. Bari Weiss, "The Self-Silencing Majority: In Red America and Blue America, an Epidemic of Self-Censorship Is Threatening Democracy," *Deseret News*, March 2, 2021.

39. United States Courts, "What Does Free Speech Mean?" accessed June 1, 2021, https://www.uscourts.gov/about-federal-courts/educational-resources/about-educational-outreach/activity-resources/what-does.

40. Voltaire, in *The Portable Voltaire,* edited by Ben Ray Redman (New York: Penguin, 1977), ebook.

41. George Lucas, *Star Wars: Episode VI - Return of the Jedi,* 20th Century Studios, May 25, 1983, https://www.youtube.com/watch?v=jZ6nF6JKtRc.

42. Tasneem Nashrulla, "The Woman Who Famously Forgave a Teen for Nearly Killing Her in a Frozen Turkey Prank Has Died," *Buzzfeed News,* March 28, 2019.

43. Ibid.

44. Abraham Lincoln, in Ronald C. White Jr, "Honest Abe Reminds Us of the Power of Our Words," NPR, March 4, 2011, https://www.npr.org/2011/03/04/134162178/150-years-later-lincolns-words-still-resonate.

45. Ibid.

46. Thomas Jefferson, in Linton Weeks, "Thomas Jefferson's 10 Rules of Life—Mocked," NPR, November 25, 2015, https://www.npr.org/sections/npr-history-dept/2015/11/05/454845747/skewering-jefferson-s-10-rules-to-live-by-19th-century-style.

47. David Robson, "Cultivating More Control over Our Lungs Can Bring Many Benefits to Our Mental and Physical Health: Is It Time to Relearn Breathing?" BBC, March 2, 2020, https://www.bbc.com/worklife/article/20200303-why-slowing-your-breathing-helps-you-relax.

48. Jenna Fletcher, "How to Use 4-7-8 Breathing for Anxiety," *Medical News Today,* February 12, 2019, https://www.medicalnewstoday.com/articles/324417#apps.

49. Ibid.

50. Paul Sonderegger, "Forget the Turing Test—Give AI the F. Scott Fitzgerald Test Instead," *Quartz,* May 21, 2018, https://www.yahoo.com/news/forget-turing-test-ai-f-110031712.html.

51. Stephen R. Covey, *The Seven Habits of Highly Effective People* (Free Press: 1989).

52. Martin Luther King, "Loving Your Enemies," delivered at Dexter Avenue Baptist Church, Montgomery, Alabama, on November 17, 1957, published in *The Martin Luther King, Jr.,* Stanford Research and Education Institute at Stanford University.

53. V. Neil Wyrick, *The Spiritual Abraham Lincoln* (Carlsbad, CA: Mangus Press, 2004), 5.

54. Mother Teresa, in John Scally, *Mother Teresa: The Irish Connection* (Dublin Ireland: Poolbeg Press Ltd., 2016), ebook, https://www.google.com/books/edition/Mother_Teresa_The_Irish_Connection/pfYiDAAAQBAJ?hl=en&gbpv=0.

55. These words are engraved on the statue of King in the District of Columbia, National Park Service, https://www.nps.gov/mlkm/learn/quotations.htm.

56. Ny Magee, "ESPN's Sage Steele Says Black Anchors Excluded Her from 'Race' Special," *The Grio*, July 21, 2020.

57. Ibid.

58. Ibid.

59. Ibid.

60. Stephen Hawkins, Daniel Yudkin, Miriam Juan-Torres, and Tim Dixon, *Hidden Tribes: A Study of America's Polarized Landscape* (New York: More in Common.com, 2018), https://hiddentribes.us/media/qfpekz4g/hidden_tribes_report.pdf.

61. John Shattuck, "We See the Left. We See the Right. Can Anyone See the 'Exhausted Majority'?" *New York Times*, March 24, 2021, https://www.nytimes.com/2021/03/24/opinion/Democrats-Republicans-left-right-center.html.

62. Stephen Hawkins, Daniel Yudkin, Miriam Juan-Torres, and Tim Dixon, *Hidden Tribes: A Study of America's Polarized Landscape* (New York: More in Common.com, 2018), https://hiddentribes.us/media/qfpekz4g/hidden_tribes_report.pdf.

63. John Shattuck, "We See the Left. We See the Right. Can Anyone See the 'Exhausted Majority'?" *New York Times*, March 24, 2021, https://www.nytimes.com/2021/03/24/opinion/Democrats-Republicans-left-right-center.html.

64. Ibid.

65. John Halpin, Brian Katulis, Peter Juul, Karl Agne, and Nish Jain, "How Americans Envision a More Perfect Union: A Common Path Forward for the Country," Center for American Progress, May 26, 2021, https://www.americanprogress.org/article/americans-envision-perfect-union/.

66. Larry Kramer, "Listening to the People Who Think We Are Wrong," Hewlett Foundation, January 10, 2019, https://hewlett.org/listening-with-empathy/.

67. Ibid.

68. Julia Rozovsky, "The Five Keys to a Successful Google Team," re:Work, November 17, 2015, https://rework.withgoogle.com/blog/five-keys-to-a-successful-google-team/.

69. Ibid.

70. Geoff Edgers, "Sarah Silverman Just Wants to Make Things Right," *Washington Post,* February 4, 2021, https://www.washingtonpost.com/arts-entertainment/2021/02/04/sarah-silverman-podcast-platform/?arc404=true.

71. Ibid.

72. Bill Donahue, "This Rural Liberal Set Out to Talk to His Pro-Trump Neighbors," *Washington Post,* February 4, 2021, https://www.washingtonpost.com/magazine/2021/02/25/this-rural-liberal-set-out-talk-his-pro-trump-neighbors/.

73. Alex Cabrero, "West Jordan Neighbors with Opposite Political Views Find Unity," *Deseret News*: November 6, 2020, https://www.deseret.com/utah/2020/11/6/21552962/news-west-jordan-neighbors-with-opposite-political-views-find-unity-trump-biden-lawn-signs.

74. Amanpour & Co., *Daryl Davis on Befriending Members of the KKK,* PBS, December 11, 2019, https://www.pbs.org/wnet/amanpour-and-company/video/daryl-davis-on-befriending-members-of-the-kkk/.

75. "Grokking Trumpists: Converting KKK Members," December 20, 2020, https://www.dailykos.com/stories/2020/12/20/1988416/-Grokking-Trumpists-Converting-KKK-Members.

76. Amanpour & Co., *"Daryl Davis on Befriending Members of the KKK,* PBS, December 11, 2019, https://www.pbs.org/wnet/amanpour-and-company/video/daryl-davis-on-befriending-members-of-the-kkk/.

77. Ibid.

78. *Mister Rogers Goes to Washington,* PBS, November 22, 2019, https://www.pbs.org/video/mister-rogers-goes-washington-ycjrnx/.

79. Arizona State University, Center for the Study of Race and Democracy, "MLK," August 16, 2011, https://csrd.asu.edu/content/mlk#:~:text=%22Violence%20begets%20violence%3B%20hate%20begets,%22%20%2DMartin%20Luther%20King%20Jr.

80. Wikipedia, s.v. "Metanoia," last modified April 26, 2022, https://en.wikipedia.org/wiki/Metanoia_(theology).

81. Mohana Basu, "Polite, Unofficial Warnings Can Reduce Hate Speech on Twitter, New York University Study Finds," *The Print*, November 23, 2021, https://theprint.in/tech/polite-unoffi-cial-warnings-can-reduce-hate-speech-on-twitter-new-york-uni-versity-study-finds/770199/.

82. Ibid.

Thanks so much for taking the time to read *The Ruby Rule*. I hope this book resonates with you and makes you a bit softer, slower to judge, and kinder. And should you err, I hope this book inspires you to fall on the side of mercy instead of justice. I want you to know that I, too, am still learning these concepts. I often fall short and hear my wife telling me to walk my own talk. If you've found even a small part of this read beneficial to you, it would mean a great deal if you could leave me a review wherever fine books are sold—and, of course, spread the word!

With sincere appreciation,
Art

ABOUT THE AUTHOR

Best-selling author, dynamic speaker, and leadership guru Arthur F. Coombs III brings decades of global expertise to readers, audiences, and corporations through his creative and innovative practices.

Founder and CEO of KomBea Corporation, Art has served for more than twenty years developing and marketing tools that blend human intelligence and automation. Art's best-selling book, *Don't Just Manage—Lead!*, has been hailed by some of the nation's top executives. His second book, *Human Connection: How the "L" Do We Do That?*, provides a powerful formula for deep and meaningful connections with others. His third best-selling book, *Hard Easy: A Get-Real Guide for Getting the Life You Want*, teaches the groundbreaking law of Hard Easy—why it's better to put in the effort now and reap the rewards later. He also created the corresponding workbook, *Living the Law of*

Hard Easy Workbook: A Get-Real Workbook for Getting the Life You Want, so that people can put the lessons in the book into practical use. Finally, expanding on the lessons from his previous books comes another book to teach a life-changing lesson: *The Ruby Rule: How More Listening and Less Labeling, Brings More Healing and Less Hating.*

Before founding KomBea, Art served as EVP of Strategic Initiatives for FirstSource. As CEO and founder of Echopass Corporation, he helped build the world's premier contact-center hosting environment. In addition, Art has served as Sento Corporation's CEO, managing director, and vice president of Europe for Sykes Enterprises, and has worked for organizations such as Hewlett-Packard, VLSI Research, and RasterOps.

Art's vast experience with people and organizations has led him to share transformative principles for creating a remarkable life—principles you can now access within these pages.

Made in United States
Troutdale, OR
07/13/2023

11192858R00159